HERE'S LITTLE R

T0001678

Forthcoming in the series:

and many more . . .

Here's Little Richard

33⅓

Jordan Bassett

BLOOMSBURY ACADEMIC
NEW YORK • LONDON • OXFORD • NEW DELHI • SYDNEY

BLOOMSBURY ACADEMIC
Bloomsbury Publishing Inc
1385 Broadway, New York, NY 10018, USA
50 Bedford Square, London, WC1B 3DP, UK
29 Earlsfort Terrace, Dublin 2, Ireland

BLOOMSBURY, BLOOMSBURY ACADEMIC and the Diana logo are trademarks of
Bloomsbury Publishing Plc

First published in the United States of America 2023

Library of Congress Cataloging-in-Publication Data

Names: Bassett, Jordan, author.
Title: Here's Little Richard / Jordan Bassett.
Description: New York: Bloomsbury Academic, 2023. | Series: 33 1/3; 179 |
Includes bibliographical references. | Summary: "The story of how the
self-proclaimed King and Queen of Rock'n'roll's explosive debut album
changed the world in 28 minutes and 30 seconds"– Provided by publisher.
Identifiers: LCCN 2023014046 (print) | LCCN 2023014047 (ebook) |
ISBN 9781501389115 (paperback) | ISBN 9781501389122 (epub) |
ISBN 9781501389139 (pdf) | ISBN 9781501389146 (ebook other)
Subjects: LCSH: Little Richard, 1932-2020. Here's Little Richard. |
Rock music–United States–To 1961–History and criticism.
Classification: LCC ML420.L773 B37 2023 (print) | LCC ML420.L773 (ebook) |
DDC 782.42166092–dc23/eng/20230406
LC record available at https://lccn.loc.gov/2023014046
LC ebook record available at https://lccn.loc.gov/2023014047

ISBN: PB: 978-1-5013-8911-5
ePDF: 978-1-5013-8913-9
eBook: 978-1-5013-8912-2

Series: 33 ⅓

Typeset by Deanta Global Publishing Services, Chennai, India
Printed and bound in Great Britain

To find out more about our authors and books visit www.bloomsbury.com
and sign up for our newsletters.

For my wonderful Grandma Rita,
the Architect of it all

With special thanks to

Kelly Lee Blackwell
Dave Grohl
Joan Jett
Sir Elton John
Sir Tom Jones
Nile Rodgers
Candi Staton
Billy Vera

Contents

Track list

'Tutti Frutti'
'True, Fine Mama'
'Can't Believe You Wanna Leave'
'Ready Teddy'
'Baby'
'Slippin' and Slidin''
'Long Tall Sally'
'Miss Ann'
'Oh Why?'
'Rip It Up'
'Jenny, Jenny'
'She's Got It'

'He was just wild'

Prologue

Little Richard was the most significant cultural figure of the twentieth century. The man who justifiably dubbed himself the Architect of Rock'n'roll was a direct influence on Elvis Presley (who nicked his songs and made them worse), the Beatles (who learned how to '*Hoo!*' directly from the source) and David Bowie (who took his iconic gender-bending into another dimension). Without Little Richard, the world would be a very different place.

It's no exaggeration to say that all contemporary pop music, with those seminal artists as his conduit, bears Richard Penniman's influence in one way or other. From male bisexuality to religion in pop, he spent the 1950s pioneering ideas that are *still* too challenging for the mainstream. He was the most exciting person on the planet between 1955 and 1957, caked in Pancake 31 make-up, his waxy pompadour piled high, his leg splayed up on the piano as he belted out tracks that channelled his fondness – and there's no delicate way to put this – for dogging and bumming.

That wild timeline is bookended by his sensational first smash 'Tutti Frutti' and his shock decision to reject rock'n'roll in favour of God, when he claimed, at the height of his fame (and erroneously, it transpired), to be quitting show business for good. In this era, Little Richard electrified stadium-sized audiences, scored thirteen brain-shaking top ten hits, became the world's most transgressive movie star and recorded the show-stoppers that make up *Here's Little Richard*, his debut album and definitive statement.

After his first dazzling burst of fame waned, though, Richard remained in the shadows for decades, loitering on the fringes of pop history, watching from afar at the chaos he'd caused, never truly receiving his due. Why? Because he was Black, queer, poor, disabled – and all of this in a society that despised every one of those words? Richard Penniman rose above the prejudice he faced to do anything he wanted, and what he wanted to do was make majestic nonsense. '*Wop-bop-aloo-bop-alop-bom-bom!*' he roared in the opening moments of 'Tutti Frutti', a joyous manifesto we could all still live by.

When the greatest rock star of all time died on 9 May 2020, at the age of eighty-seven, Sir Paul McCartney tweeted: 'Little Richard came screaming into my life when I was a teenager. I owe a lot of what I do to Little Richard and his style; and he knew it.' The Beatles opened for their idol at the Hamburg Star-Club in 1962; it was here that Richard taught the Fab Four his raucous vocal tic. In that tweet, Macca recalled: 'He would say, "I taught Paul everything he knows." I had to admit he was right.'

Dave Grohl, the Foo Fighters frontman and former drummer of Nirvana, arguably the greatest rock'n'roller of his *own* generation, is also indebted to Little Richard. 'To me, he embodied the true spirit of rock'n'roll', Grohl says. 'I do consider him to be the originator – the Architect – because you have to imagine the adversities he was faced with, socially, at the time. He was coming out as this outrageous, flamboyant entertainer and . . . you know, he was just wild.'

Sir Elton John, meanwhile, explains that Richard was a major catalyst in his own career: 'The way he looked, and the voice, and the fact that he beat shit out of [the piano]. . . . He changed my life. Elvis I loved, but when Little Richard came out and started playing that piano – boy, oh boy! I knew exactly what I wanted to do.' The Rocket Man adds with a grin: 'I didn't know it would turn out so well!'

Joan Jett grew up listening to Little Richard, thanks to her brother, who is a massive music fan, while her partner is a '50s culture buff. And, of course, she is a rock'n'roll icon herself: 'It is impossible to be in the world I'm in and not be in contact with Little Richard's music and persona', she points out. Upon his death, Jett also tweeted a tribute to the man she called 'THE ORIGINAL GLAM ROCKER'. Asked to define that memorable phrase, she says: 'He had the glitter, the glam, and wasn't afraid to be "different". He wore his rock'n'roll clothes like armour, and so did I.'

And Richard certainly needed armour. A typically problematic John Lennon recalled the moment he and his school pals first heard 'Long Tall Sally' round a fellow Elvis Presley fan's house in the mid-1950s: 'It was so great I couldn't speak . . . I didn't want to leave Elvis, but this was so much better. . . . How could they *both* be happening in my life? And then someone said, "It's a n*****r singing." I didn't know negroes sang. So Elvis was white and Little Richard was black. This was a great relief. "Thank you, God," I said. "There is a difference between them.'"

This unnecessarily ugly recollection points to the racial barriers Little Richard ploughed a piano through. The success of *Here's Little Richard*, which was released in March 1957 and spent five weeks on *Billboard's* Best-Selling Pop Albums chart, occurred less than two years after Rosa Parks refused to give up her seat on that bus in Montgomery, Alabama. It also arrived seven years before the Civil Rights Act of 1964 theoretically quashed the last of the racist, segregationist Jim Crow laws that blighted the American South for nearly a century.

As David Kirby noted in *Little Richard: The Birth of Rock 'n' Roll*, it was only three weeks prior to the recording of 'Tutti Frutti' that Emmett Till, a fourteen-year-old Black boy, was murdered in Mississippi for allegedly flirting with a white woman. Till's lynching, a major catalyst in the Civil Rights Movement, throws into even starker relief the danger that Richard himself flirted as a hyper-sexualized Black entertainer with a predominantly white audience.

By his own explanation, his cartoonish appearance was a means of survival, of making himself palatable to a world that was not yet ready for Little Richard. He softened himself so as not to seem threatening to an American mainstream that still clung to the concept of white supremacy. And it worked. Although he claimed his audiences were '90 per cent' white in the *Here's Little Richard* era, it's also true that this unifying force quite literally pulled down the barrier between his Black-and-white fans, who would defy segregation and dance together to his stellar tunes.

Richard limped because he had one leg longer than the other, which led neighbours to brand him effeminate when he was child, and it's bitterly ironic that this shunned outsider would so singularly shape the entirety of modern mainstream popular culture in his image. And yet there was something almost inevitable about Little Richard, as though the planet's tectonic plates had shifted with the sole purpose of forming his stage.

He was, after all, not completely without precedent. The young Richard Penniman, as we shall see, was inspired by proto-rock'n'rollers such as Arkansas party starter Louis Jordan and, closer to home, his drag queen pal Esquerita, whose heavily made-up look and pompadour wig Richard would appropriate to iconic effect. He was also a product of the queer underground that thrived beneath the surface in his hometown of Macon, Georgia; in the tell-all 1984 biography *The Life and Times of Little Richard*, he recounted his early sexual experiences with both men and women in a level of detail that can only be described as 'eye-watering'. When these heady influences collided with the steamrolling rock'n'roll movement, which gathered pace with a Memphis mama's boy and a Louisiana piano-pounder at the helm, all hell broke loose.

Elvis and Jerry Lee Lewis might have battled with the tension between rock'n'roll and religion, but Little Richard took the struggle to the extreme. In October 1957, onstage at the Sydney Stadium, the 24-year-old superstar informed 40,000 incensed fans that he was turning his back on the Devil's tunes. He would instead become a Christian evangelist. Here, again, Richard was radically ahead of the world. There was general disbelief when, in 2019, Kanye West claimed he'd quit secular music to make only gospel records. Really, though – like so many others and in so many ways – he was following the lead of his '50s predecessor.

Richard claimed his conversion to be the will of God Himself. It was a long time before WhatsApp, so God sent the message in the form of a blazing fireball that rocketed through the night sky in Sydney, which our hero spotted from the stage. He shrugged off the remaining ten days of his two-week tour, and the ensuing lawsuits, insisting he'd now focus only on his higher purpose. The reality proved a little more complex – Richard Penniman's righteousness was matched only by the rock star contrariness of Little Richard, who would be back on the road in Europe, blasting through 'Tutti Frutti', by October 1962. Yet he never quite recaptured the reckless abandon of his cosmic debut. Well, who could?

In fact, it's almost as if Richard Penniman was only *really* Little Richard for the two years in which its twelve molten tunes were recorded and toured, as though he'd been possessed by some unknown force, like a rock'n'roll *Invasion of the Bodysnatchers*. The record is an awesome encapsulation of its author in this red-hot era. It is not, though, an 'album' in the modern sense. As Grammy winning music historian Billy Vera points out: 'That wasn't done in those days with rock'n'roll and rhythm and blues.' Instead studio sessions would produce both A and B-sides for singles – and, in our man's case, would later be distributed among LPs. *Here's Little Richard* is, therefore, a collection of six chart smashes and six previously unreleased studio sessions recorded between 1955 and late 1956, a 'Best of' romp that still sends out a rebel signal.

Once 'Tutti Frutti' had ripped open the vortex to a parallel universe that looked like a *Looney Tunes* animation – all wobbly lines, exclamation marks and thought bubbles filled with dreams of ballin' Saturday nights – yet more seismic tracks spilled out. The punch-drunk haze of 'Rip It Up', the desperately horny 'She's Got It', the microphone-distorting 'Jenny, Jenny': no one had ever heard anything like the raw power that oozes through these songs.

The record is also a time machine, crystallizing those early influences even as it points to the future of pop culture itself. All of its key players are now gone. Some major characters in our story – namely Richard's live drummer Charles Connor and the mogul Art Rupe, who founded Specialty Records, the label that released *Here's Little Richard* – died as this book was being written. Rupe hated interviews, leaving his friend Billy Vera, who was a consultant for the imprint from 1989 to 1995 and penned its official history *Rip It Up: The Specialty Records Story*, to do the talking for him. The founder was still alive when Vera was interviewed for these pages; the historian's references to him, in the present tense, have been kept intact. The tunes from the dawn of rock'n'roll endure, but the generation that made them is slipping away.

Luckily, our subject's life is sealed on wax: the story of *Here's Little Richard* is the story of the Architect himself. And to understand what might just be the greatest record ever made, we must first understand where Richard Penniman himself came from – his unusual childhood, his own influences and his route to stardom – along with the immediate impact of this record's sonic explosions and the tremors in the years that followed.

Even in the early '60s, as he made faltering attempts to recreate the outrage of the late '50s, Little Richard was iconoclastic. It was right there in his beloved mirrored jacket (which prophesised the mirrored jumpsuit that Harry Styles melted the internet with at Coachella festival in 2022). It was right there, too, in the sequin-studded flares, in the eyelashes that grew longer and the make-up that became ever-more camp, answering the question he purred through in an early version of his debut's album track 'Baby': 'Don't you wish your man looked like Little Richard?'. If David Bowie brought Britain to a standstill by unveiling the sexy, androgynous Ziggy Stardust on *Top of the Pops* in 1972, remember that the originator wore a quasi-Pope robe to a gig in Doncaster, northern England, in 1962.

Bowie himself said on American television in 1991: 'Without [Little Richard], I think myself and half of my contemporaries wouldn't be playing music.' Since Prince didn't really do humble, it was left to Penniman to point out the debt the Purple One owed him: 'Prince is the Little Richard of his generation', he insisted in another US television interview in 1989, before turning to the camera to exclaim to his imitator: 'I was wearing purple before you was wearing it!'

Little Richard was so transgressive it's almost impossible to imagine he existed, and yet his influence is so unparalleled it's equally impossible to imagine the world without him. In the decades that followed *Here's Little Richard*, during his many returns to the mainstream, he eulogized himself with colourful nicknames: the Georgia Peach, the Living Flame, the Quasar, the Southern Child. 'I am the Creator!' he exclaimed. 'The Originator! The emancipator! I am the *One*!' Best and most accurately of all, he crowned himself the King and Queen of Rock'n'roll.

Nile Rodgers shared many a chat show green room with Richard in the '80s and '90s. In this period, the disco don says, 'It was just important for him to walk into the room and sit down and say, "Oh! I did this first, and I did that."' Draped in lamé, his pencil moustache pristine, now wearing wigs that towered taller his pompadour ever did, his demeanour chaotic, Little Richard spent these appearances marvelling at the magic he'd sprinkled across the globe, as if couldn't quite believe it himself.

But how on Earth did we get here?

'The greatest intro ever'

1
The Big Bang

There are plenty of gigs that purportedly changed the world. The Stones at Altamont: bloodshed, mayhem, chaos and the death of a utopian dream. The Pistols at the Manchester Lesser Free Trade Hall: spit, snot, sweat and the messy birth of a revolution. Yet the only gig that *truly* changed the world occurred in 1955, at a beat-up shack extended from a barbershop in New Orleans, when an exhausted singer and his frustrated producer took a recording break to wet their whistles at the Dew Drop Inn.

Richard Penniman, a 22-year-old dishwasher, had cut a few derivative records by the mid-1950s; forgettable R&B numbers that pitched him as a laconic crooner in the vein of Louisiana legend Lloyd Price. But by 1957, he had somehow metamorphozed into the mercurial and outrageous Little Richard, an openly bisexual multimillionaire rock star who, the gospel funkster Bobby Byrd once claimed, was so flush with cash he kept a mountain of loose notes in the trunk of his car.

And the transformation occurred, in an instant, at the Dew Drop on 14 September 1955, when he belted out 'Tutti Frutti' – along with its original, unprintable lyrics: 'Tutti Frutti, good booty / If it don't fit, don't force it / You can grease it, make it easy.' The ground split in two, and the Devil rose up, flashed his forked tongue and declared the godless days of rock'n'roll officially underway.

~

At least, that's the most popular – and entertaining – version of the story, which was laid out in *The Life and Times of Little Richard*, an authorized tome that saw author Charles White invite the Quasar and producer Robert 'Bumps' Blackwell to relay their tall tale. And, if you're sitting comfortably, it goes a little like this.

One of those middling R&B tunes had given Richard Penniman – a man, it would transpire, with an addictive personality – a taste for fame. The smoochy, self-penned 'Every Hour', recorded in Atlanta in late 1951, became a big local hit in Macon and in the wider state of Georgia. It was also a mainstay on the jukebox at the Tip In Inn, a Macon watering hole managed by his domineering father, Charles 'Bud' Penniman. Bolstered by his brief success, and the endorsement of a parent with whom his relationship was complex at best, the wannabe star mailed out an audition tape to the LA-based Specialty Records, whom he spent the best part of 1955 pestering for a session.

Upon listening to Richard's compelling – if naïve – audition tape, which consisted of the winsome 'Wonderin'' and the treacly 'He's My Star', Art Rupe eventually relented and sent the inexperienced Blackwell to meet the singer at J&M Recording Studio in New Orleans. 'When I walked in', the producer recalled, 'there's this cat in this loud shirt, with hair waved up six inches above his head. He was talking wild, thinking up stuff just to be different, you know? I could tell he was a mega-personality.'

Today, Kelly Lee Blackwell says there was an instant connection between the Georgia Peach and her late father, who co-produced *Here's Little Richard* with Art Rupe: 'They just clicked really well because, I think, they had the same mindset of: "This is great music that we're going to put out. We are going to change the world musically – we're going to put [out] something that no-one has ever heard." My father saw Richard as: "I know this man is going to be *great*. I can see it."'

The music they produced in that initial six-hour session, though, was in little danger of changing the world. 'He's My Star' was so saccharine that Blackwell didn't even bother to record it, while 'The Most I Can Offer' came out similarly sugary. At least 'Wonderin'' was upbeat. Where was the chaos reported at the wild-talkin' performer's electric, anarchic live shows?

'It wasn't going well at J&M', notes Kelly Lee. 'It just wasn't having that *funk*.' Blackwell himself recalled: 'In the studio that day, [Richard] was very inhibited.'

It's a testament to the vocalist and producer that each of these recordings later found a home. The latter two appeared on the cobbled-together album *The Fabulous Little Richard*, which was released after he'd left rock'n'roll. Rupe clamped girl group harmonies, provided by the Stewart Sisters, a Californian trio, onto the tunes to fill them out – and it somehow sounds fantastic. 'He's My Star', meanwhile, finally surfaced with a lusher sound on his sacred 1961 record *The King of the Gospel Singers*. The song's a heartbreaker, but you can understand why Blackwell didn't see it doing much damage to the *Billboard* charts.

The producer was frustrated, and the clock was ticking. So he and Richard hit upon a solution that has offered inspiration to millions of people with a problem in the decades before and since: they went down the pub.

And lo: ensconced in the spit-and-sawdust surrounds of the Dew Drop Inn, the Quasar-in-waiting was suddenly loose enough to unlock the manic energy Blackwell had heard so much about. Now he had an audience to impress, Little Richard was ready to rip it up, to jump onstage and bash out the song that would change everything, kickstart the rock'n'roll revolution and light the fuse that blazed through '70s punk, '80s hip hop and everything that followed.

Blackwell remembered: 'He hits that piano – *didididididididididididi!* – and starts to sing, *"A-wop-bop-a-loo-mop a-good-goddamn! / Tutti frutti – good booty!"* I said, "Wow! That's what I want from you, Richard. That's a hit!"'

'When Richard started bangin',' says Kelly Lee, 'that was the key to it. It was a different type of funk goin' on when Richard started pounding on the piano and singing. Richard had a certain style about him and daddy just had to pull that out of him for that song.'

And so Richard and Bumps raced back to the studio, pushed the big red button with fifteen minutes of the session remaining and bottled black magic, released 'Tutti Frutti' and sent Planet Earth on a collision course with eternal damnation.

But wait.

~

Here we must lift the needle from the record. *Vrrrrffft!* This account, as we'll explore in Chapter 8, has been contested by one Dorothy LaBostrie, the songwriter with whom Richard Wayne Penniman shares a credit on 'Tutti Frutti'. And it's far from the only conflicting testimony in the tale of *Here's Little Richard*.

Throughout our story, the truth is as fluid as the Architect's sexuality; for every anecdote, there may be a handful of parallel viewpoints. In his Beatles biography *One Two Three Four: The Beatles in Time*, Craig Brown quotes Paul McCartney as having said of the Fab Four phenomenon: 'In an earthquake, you get many different versions of what happened by all the people that saw it. And they're all true.' So, pick one.

And the earthquake analogy couldn't be more appropriate for the Dew Drop Inn yarn, which represents a massive cultural rupture. The story is irresistible in that it speaks so directly to the endlessly fascinating combination of ego and insecurity that's marked many a superstar in decades since Specialty Records released 'Tutti Frutti'. Richard harboured a deep *need* to perform. How, then, could he be, in Blackwell's recollection, 'inhibited' in the studio?

This, after all, is the man who became one of the most unforgettable entertainers in pop history. As Candi Staton, the singer of the 1976 disco smash 'Young Hearts Run Free', who was well acquainted with the Southern Child, puts it: 'You moved somethin' when Little Richard was onstage! You moved your toes, your fingers. You moved somethin'! That beat, the way he presented it . . . it was just *there* and you had to move!'

Perhaps, though, the young Richard Penniman so craved fame that he was frozen, afraid to let loose in case he blew his big opportunity. After mailing his audition tape to Art Rupe, he had spent eight long months toiling away in the kitchen, awaiting the call that would finally make America wake up to the majesty flowing through him. Blackwell speculated that the lukewarm tunes they initially recorded found his fledgling star, who'd been reared on gospel, emphasizing the 'spiritual feeling' that had always proved such a crowd-pleaser for him.

Maybe, too, he was overawed by the J&M studio that day. Its session players – including saxophonist Lee Allen and bassist Frank Fields – were New Orleans legends who regularly backed iconic R&B star Fats Domino; beneath the loud shirt, the waved-up hair and the stuff he said just to be different, he was little more than a 22-year-old local boy who was a long way home.

'[J&M] was an incredible studio', says Kelly Lee. 'There was a certain sound that was coming out of that studio that drew artists like Fats and Ike and Tina Turner and Lloyd [Price] and so many others. Sometimes I think some places just have magic in 'em.'

If Richard Penniman did feel out of his depth at J&M, which was rudimentary by modern standards but slick compared to WBML, the Macon radio station in which he'd recorded the early versions of 'Wonderin'' and 'He's My Star', he'd be more at home at the Dew Drop Inn. It was Little Richard's kind of place.

~

The Black-owned venue was a hotbed of African-American talent, attracting the likes of Tennessee titan Big Maybelle and a fledgling James Brown. It was also something of a queer mecca, hosting the annual Halloween Gay Ball emceed by local 'female impersonator' – to use the parlance of the day – Patsy Vidalia. A formidable master of ceremonies, Vidalia rocked pancake make-up and shimmering ballgowns – looks that Richard will have recognized from queer underground Macon, which had nurtured his own fabulous drag alter-ego, Princess Lavonne. (The chaotic Lavonne burned brightly and briefly in his younger years – more of which later.)

Indeed, released from the pressure of the studio and among his people at the Dew Drop in late 1955, as per the legend, Richard Penniman was free to *become* Little Richard. 'They were more relaxed [there] 'cause they were chillin'', says Kelly Lee Blackwell. 'Everybody would go there and once they could relax and flow with it, it just kinda came.'

Billy Vera, who also endorses the official rendition of the tale, emphasizes Richard's affinity with a joint like the Dew Drop Inn: '[He] gets up on the piano at the Dew Drop and starts showing off, doing this dirty song that he used to do

– he played a lot of these college dates for drunken college boys, and they liked hearing dirty songs. That was their idea of a good time.' The tune appealed to another audience, too: 'When he would be in drag, that would be generally at a black nightclub. He sometimes worked that way, and so he'd sing that song: *"Tutti Fruitti / Good booty . . . A wop bop a loo bop A GOOD GOD DAMN".*'

Just imagine how Bumps Blackwell, whom Art Rupe had instructed to extract magic from Richard and who had thus far mined only mediocrity, would feel when he heard that sensational but unreleasable ode to bum sex. And picture Richard roaring through those X-rated lyrics, standing up at the grimy old piano in this sweat-stained bar, surrounded by the freaks and misfits who formed his congregation, almost drowned out by the whoops that were their hallelujahs.

The rookie producer was keen to impress Art Rupe, who'd taken a chance on him. Blackwell was already 'nervous', says Vera, by the time they arrived at the Dew Drop: 'He'd spent all this money on a session with six or seven musicians and had to answer to his boss, and he clearly didn't come up with a hit in that first session in the morning.' So Richard's version of 'Tutti Frutti' posed a conundrum. 'If it don't fit, don't force it' – pardon? 'You can grease it, make it easy' – come again? This was sixty-five years before Cardi B and Megan Thee Stallion appalled right-wing commentators with the sex-positive 'WAP'. If they'd recited Richard's lyrics in 2020, they would still have raised eyebrows.

'They wouldn't have gotten any airplay with the way the lyrics were at the time', points out Kelly Lee, whose father was already working on a game plan. This is where Dorothy

LaBostrie, whose 'Tutti Frutti' story so diverges from the canonical narrative, enters the scene. Blackwell claimed he simply asked her to rewrite its naughty words; she reckoned she contributed rather more to the planet-warping tune. Either way, that 'good booty' became 'aw rootie!', raunchy Richard's paean to lubricated carnality hosed down into a radio-ready rocker about gals named Daisy and Sue, both of them as wholesome as a strawberry milkshake down the five-and-dime.

'Tutti Frutti', though, retains its transgressive energy, the naughtiness of its origin bristling in every note. And that's not to mention Richard's A-grade genius a capella intro, an explosive drum solo performed without an instrument and an homage to the rock music movement that didn't even exist yet. The song is nothing less than a rip in the space-time continuum, and it brought the onset of modern music rushing in on 1955.

'I think the greatest intro of a record ever was "Tutti Frutti"', beams Elton John, who ecstatically imitates the musician he's called his 'biggest influence': '"*Wop-bop-aloo-bop-alop-bom-bom!*" You can't beat that!'

~

Little Richard admitted to Charles White in 1984:

> I'd been singing 'Tutti Frutti' for years, but it never struck me as a song you'd *record*. I didn't go to New Orleans to record no 'Tutti Frutti'. Sure, it used to crack the crows up when I sang it in the clubs, with those risqué lyrics. . . .

But I never thought it would be a hit, even with the lyrics cleaned up.

That dirty song was a hit, all right, reaching number two on the *Billboard* R&B chart and crossing over to number twenty-one on the pop chart. Specialty shifted a staggering 200,000 copies of 'Tutti Frutti' within ten days of its release. By 1968, the track had achieved three million sales in America alone. 'When it was released, it was magical', says Billy Vera, who explains that zeitgeist-chasing radio DJs clamoured to spin the tune in 1955: 'I mean, it was one of those automatic hits. Everybody wanted to play it.'

Richard claimed to have been oblivious to the song's immediate success and explained that he was 'sittin' in Macon, broke with no money' when Specialty called, demanding he jump on a plane – his first ever – to attend Hollywood's Radio Recorders, Inc., studio for the follow-up.

Here, in late November, just over two months after he'd played the gig that changed the world at the Dew Drop Inn, he recorded five tunes that eventually made the cut for *Here's Little Richard* (albeit some in different forms). These were the early stages of the album that vacuum-packed his gigantic persona into twenty-eight minutes and thirty seconds of sex, revelry, teenage rebellion . . . and more sex.

'I'm gonna be a superstar!'

2
Macon, Georgia

Richard claimed that the story of 'Tutti Frutti' went back to the Greyhound Bus Station kitchen in Macon. 'I was washing dishes', he said in a blockbusting *Rolling Stone* comeback cover interview in 1970. 'I couldn't talk back to my boss man. He would bring all these pots back for me to wash, and one day I said, "I've got to do something to stop this man bringing back all these pots to me to wash," and I said, "Awap bop a lup bop a wop bam boom – take 'em out!"'

The lyric is also drawn from the raw musicality that permeated every part of life in Macon – thanks, largely, to the expressive church singers whose congregation could be heard for blocks with no amplification. More specifically, it's been suggested that 'a-wop-bop-a-loo-bop-a-lop-bam-boom' channels Bamalama, a one-eyed washboard player he recalled ringing a schoolteacher's bell around town, singing, 'A-bamalam, you shall be free / And in the mornin' you shall be free.'

This idea bottles the essence of Little Richard's persona, as it relays his lifelong bid to be free – personally, in terms of the liberation offered by rock'n'roll, and collectively as part of the church – and does so with a bit of narrative mythmaking. It's perfectly fitting that in 1964, attempting to recapture the wildness of 'Tutti Frutti' after years away from the mainstream, he released a self-penned track called 'Bama Lama Bama Loo'. Unfortunately, it sounds like an AI bot wrote a Little Richard song.

He also claimed to have written 'Long Tall Sally', a standout from his cosmic debut, in that kitchen – though, to continue a theme, this is in dispute (thanks to a figure whose identity remained a secret for nearly sixty years and will be revealed later in our tale). Either way, a tapestry of elements from Penniman's pre-superstar years appear to come together on *Here's Little Richard*, be it poor old Bamalama on 'Tutti Frutti' or Richard's friend and benefactor Ann Howard on the bluesy 'Miss Ann'. It's as though these characters hopped aboard the fame train with him and found themselves in for a hell of a ride.

'Slippin' and Slidin'', meanwhile, with its 'peepin' and a-hidin'', suggestively invokes the erotic adventurers he would watch having sex in a car about town. This is an evocation of Macon's aforementioned queer underground, occupied as it was by the likes of Bobby, a gender-fluid friend who seduced soldiers at Kentucky's Fort Campbell army base in exchange for cold, hard cash.

~

All of which was a long way from 1540 Fifth Avenue, a one-storey house in Pleasant Hill, the unpaved but relatively salubrious African-American neighbourhood that Richard Penniman was born into on 5 December 1932. Prior to managing a moonshine operation alongside the Tip In Inn, his father was a brickmason. Bud was not a man of distinction, but Richard's mother, Leva Mae, hailed from an educated and wealthy family, her sophistication evident in the fact that her own father's house contained a proper bath with running water.

Richard recalled: 'We weren't a poor family and we weren't a rich family. . . We didn't beg. We went to school dressed neat. Our house was clean and at Christmas we had everything.'

His life, however, began with a mistake: Bud and Leva Mae intended to call their son Ricardo Penniman, but the registrar misspelled the name. If it seems strange that they chose to live with the gaffe, they also had their hands full: Ricardo – sorry, *Richard* – was the third of twelve children. Or was it more? 'His mother said she didn't even know how many kids she had', laughs Billy Vera. 'Whether she had fourteen or fifteen kids, she didn't know.'

Yet Richard soon saw the luxuries that paved the road less travelled. Via the nightlife and naughtiness of his bar and moonshine gig, Bud filled the family home with comforts to set the Pennimans apart from their neighbours. Where most of the residents in Pleasant Hill made do with gas lamps, his and Leva Mae's house was illuminated by electric lights.

He even created a playground for his offspring, replete with slides and swings, which became the envy of white kids who lived a few streets across from the Pennimans. The temptation proved too much for some, who would cross the racial divide in order to play with Richard and his siblings. Black children could never have dared to enter a white family's garden in the ugly age of Jim Crow, of course. This grim contradiction set the template for the white revellers who packed out the venues that Richard and his all-Black live band, the Upsetters, rocked in the mid-1950s, given that the musicians were not equally free to cut loose offstage.

Bud, meanwhile, owned a Model-T Ford, the stately 1908 motor that is widely considered to be the first car that was readily available to middle-class Americans. No wonder his son soon developed a taste for shiny red Cadillacs bankrolled by taboo-busting after-hours entertainment.

Richard ached to be validated by his dad, who despised his mannerisms and allegedly feminine way of walking. Bud thrashed him for these transgressions and cruelly announced: 'My father had seven sons and I wanted seven sons. You've spoiled it – you're only half a son.' Local kids taunted him for being different, too. 'He said, "I didn't realise I was doin' it," explains Billy Vera, '"but they would call me 'punk', 'sissy', 'f****t."' Richard Penniman, though, could only be himself.

He might have enjoyed the local success of 'Every Hour', but the flashy proprietor of the Tip In Inn never saw his 'half a son' go all the way. Bud was shot and killed outside his own bar on 12 February 1952, plunging the family into poverty. A suspect was indicted in his murder, but the case was acquitted. Upon hearing the news of his father's death, Richard recalled, 'My whole body just fell out.'

It is painful to consider that Bud, so proud of his third child for achieving a Macon jukebox fixture, never heard a note of the world-changing 'Tutti Frutti' and never learned that the qualities he loathed the most were precisely what made the planet fall in love with Little Richard.

~

The budding singer had, at least, found an early fan in God Himself. In March 1957, as part of an article that announced the release of *Here's Little Richard*, the *New Musical Express* reported: 'His first real encounter with music was as a pianist and gospel singer in a Macon Sanctified Church, where he was dubbed the "War Hawk" on account of the emotional hysteria he caused among those who heard his enthusiastic singing of religious songs.'

At this tender age, Richard also joined the Tiny Tots, a kiddie gospel group who'd get together every Wednesday to recite Bible verses, sing and pray. Here he enjoyed his first taste of life as a travelling musician, as his Uncle Willard drove the kids around small Georgia towns to perform gospel standards such as 'Precious Lord' and 'Peace in the Valley' in old folks' homes, on the streets and on the steps of people's houses.

Little Richard poured this evangelical fervour into everything he did – including his '50s rock'n'roll bangers. He took on the gospel shouting he learned way down in Macon, Georgia, and transposed it into an hysterical celebration of sex, boys, girls, cars, cash and 'havin' me some fun tonight'. When the innovator passed away, the critic Tavia Nyong'o paid homage with a *Guardian* article that pointed out the stylistic parallels in passionate vocals in rock and religion. 'The separation between secular and sacred performance', Nyong'o wrote, 'might need to be bridged in order to truly appreciate the ecstasy in Little Richard's sound.'

'That's what he was', explains Sir Tom Jones, who forged an enduring friendship with his idol from the mid-1960s. 'He was a gospel singer. Like a lot of Black people were – Sam Cooke was; there was a lot of them that turned from gospel to pop music or rock music. But a lot of that is gospel roots, you know . . . rhythm and blues, blues, rock'n'roll – it's from the church.'

Richard himself said of his early years: 'There was so much poverty, so much prejudice. I imagine people had to sing to feel their connection with God. To sing their trials away, to make their burdens easier and the load lighter. That's the beginning. That's where it started.'

In Macon, he saw not only the redemptive quality of praise music but also, more prosaically, that singing might provide a life for him. This was not just a financial matter: it was also a means of transcending Pleasant Hill, a place that could not contain his enormous talent and personality. As a boy, he claimed to be a spiritual healer, reaching out to sick people who swore they felt better for his touch. Little Richard learned early on the power in giving people hope. So it's perhaps natural that, as Bumps Blackwell suspected, he would cling to this 'spiritual feeling' as a newbie in the studio.

Richard's faith helped to define his persona in his later career, too. When Elton John finally worked with his hero in 1993, the result was the gospel-infused 'The Power', which appeared on the Rocket Man's Gold-selling album of collaborations, *Duets*. 'When we knew that we were gonna write a song for Little Richard', says Elton, 'I wanted to do a gospel kind of song because I knew that's where he turned to after the rock'n'roll thing [and] he was very gospel-influenced.'

Elton's writing partner, Bernie Taupin, penned the song's lyrics with Richard's religiosity in mind. 'We walk with the power every day', the duo belt out over thunderous percussion assisted by a gospel choir and a jubilant horn section, 'Never letting the light slip away'. It is, Elton beams, 'one of my favourite tracks of all time that I've ever done'.

~

On the other hand, Richard was young, too, when he fell for the delicious fruit of secular tunes. According to that March 1957 issue of *NME*, he was fourteen when he got himself sacked from the gig as a pianist in the Macon Sanctified Church. 'Richard', the rag reported, 'was confusing religious fervour with rhythmic boogie-woogie and "barrelhouse-style" piano playing, and although Richard always had himself a ball, the congregation weren't quite so happy!'

The adolescent Richard Penniman landed his first straight job at the Macon City Auditorium, where he sold Coca-Cola to thirsty punters and experienced the power of moustachioed bandleader Cab Calloway, jump blues trumpeter Cootie Williams and – his absolute favourite –

guitar wizard Sister Rosetta Tharpe. He may have planned to be a preacher as a child, but here Little Richard saw another way to uplift people: showbiz.

At the age of seventeen, he toured Georgia with Doctor Nobilio, a local prophet who wowed audiences with a pickled human foetus adorned with horns on its head and claws for feet. He similarly became the musical entertainment for Dr Hudson's Medicine Show, accompanying the dodgy doc on his dubious mission to relieve Georgia of its aches and pains. From here Richard entered white clubs as the featured vocalist with B. Brown and his Orchestra, belting out reliable old favourites such as the Nat King Cole smoothie 'Mona Lisa'.

Perhaps, though, a stint with Sugarfoot Sam from Alabam, a travelling minstrel vaudeville troupe, was the most significant of his earliest gigs (and not just because he was now billed as 'Little Richard', an obvious allusion to his slight frame). An anachronism even at the time, this kind of minstrel show was a hangover that lingered from the preceding century.

The legacy of minstrelsy, a blatantly racist brand of 'entertainment' – a pitiful word for white performers acting out painful stereotypes in blackface – was complicated when Black performers entered the practice (or at least a version of it) around the mid-1800s. W. C. Handy, the African-American composer who lived from 1873 to 1958, described its new form, which found Black-owned troupes showcasing musical talent they could rarely earn a crust from elsewhere, as 'one of the greatest outlets for talented [Black] musicians and artists' in the late nineteenth century.

In a sublime demonstration of how much Little Richard overcame, the term 'Jim Crow' actually hailed from the name of a minstrel character played in blackface by the white performer Thomas 'Daddy' Rice. Just over a century later, having started out in minstrelsy, Richard was inspiring mixed audiences to shake off the very racist laws Rice had given a name to.

Contradictorily, too, Richard 'found' himself with Sugarfoot Sam from Alabam, whose players put on a jubilant, celebratory show. With its name emblazoned across a rickety stage and its scantily clad performers decked out in ritzy headdresses, flanked by garish illustrations of musicians at the piano and trumpet, the travelling theatre belonged to what David Kirby (lifting the phrase from Greil Marcus) has branded 'old, weird America'. This was a world of snake oil salesmen and local prophets, a 'handmade world' – in Kirby's words – of dirt and wood.

When a female cast member didn't turn up one night, Richard was told to throw on her dress. The boy with the mismatched legs tottered around in someone else's high heels and a badly fitting crimson gown. Forget the transcendently glamorous style of the show itself; this was more like the messy, punky style of drag that would emerge from '00s New York City. 'I was the biggest mess you ever saw', Richard admitted decades after the performance. 'They called me Princess Lavonne . . . I looked like the freak of the year.' There were calls for Lavonne to become a regular fixture in the Sugarfoot Sam repertoire, but Richard – perhaps wary of becoming a punchline, as he had been to those kids in childhood – hung up his dress and moved on from the show.

It's so typical, however, that he would, even if briefly, take a form of entertainment rooted in prejudice and navigate it with anarchic humour. The gig may represent the apogee of this early incarnation of our hero, a gospel-inspired, gender-bending icon-in-the-making who was still schmaltzy enough to sing a Nat King Cole song. All of these influences are evident in *Here's Little Richard*, be it in the record's frenzied vocal delivery ('Long Tall Sally'), sexual reckless abandon ('Tutti Frutti') or smooth sense of romance ('True, Fine Mama'). Sometimes, as on 'Jenny, Jenny', he combines all three.

~

In a curious twist of fate, Candi Staton knew Little Richard back in his early '50s salad days, long before she found fame and just when he was on the brink of becoming a star. 'He was such a wonderful person', she says. 'Kind – he was always kind. And he talked a lot. You never had a dull moment around Richard.'

Staton was 'twelve or thirteen' at the time, he in his 'upper teens'. She attended the Jewell Christian Academy, a religious school in Nashville, where she was one-third of the Jewell Gospel Trio. The group was managed by one Nettie Mae Harrison, whom Staton describes as 'a rebel', adding: 'She was somebody that just loved to have fun and party and go out with people and do what whatever. She was built – if I wanna quote The Commodores – like a brickhouse. She was *built*. I mean, she had a little waistline, big hips and she was about five-nine or five-ten. Tall. The way she walked was just very provocative. All the guys were attracted to her.'

Naturally, Nettie Mae and Little Richard were 'very, very close friends'. He often tagged along when the manager visited the school, whose strait-laced overseers were disapproving of her rebellious nature. Imagine, then, what they made of the Living Flame, who'd rock up in his 'pedal pushers' – rolled-up trousers – with a handkerchief pinned to one leg cuff. 'Richard was the only one I knew who wore pants like that', says Staton. 'He was fly!'

When she first met the flamboyant stranger, who would chat to the girls from the other side of the school fence, the young Candi asked Nettie Mae, 'Who is *that*?' Mae replied: 'Girl, he is amazing. He sings!' Sure enough, Richard sang and danced for the entertainment of the Jewell Gospel Trio: 'He would just make it up as he stood there – in his style, you know. We'd be pattin' our seat and clappin' our hands to him. We would harmonise with him.'

For three kids in a conservative Christian school, this was something of a thrill. 'He was our excitement!' laughs Staton. 'Every time he came through and started coming, we'd be running to the gates to him. He used to always say, "I'm gonna be a superstar!" And I'd say, "Yeah, right! You're gonna be a superstar, alright. You're a superstar now!" We used to tease him and stuff'. She adds, wistfully: 'We didn't know how that was gonna turn out, but he ended up being a superstar.'

It was a few years later, in the wake of 'Tutti Frutti', that Staton realized he'd been right all along: 'I kept hearing his name on the radio. We would turn on the radio and I'm like, "Come on now! Is that *RICHARD!?*" We were *floored*. "Little Richard! He *said* he was gon' be a star." I was like, "*That's* the dude who used to . . . He *did* get famous!"' Watching him rip it up on national television, Staton says, 'I would tell people, "Oh – I know him! We knew him before he became famous. He was just a normal person."'

You might fairly question whether Nettie Mae's funny friend in the pedal pushers, who sang his made-up songs through the fence, was ever really a 'normal person'. It's true, though, that Richard Penniman was undergoing his transformation into the taboo-busting, multimillionaire rock star Little Richard, the man who moved in magic dust.

'Music just got bigger'

3
Influences

What happened next was not simply an act of God, whatever Little Richard might tell you. 'Tutti Frutti' was the fabulously unnatural conclusion of American music mutating and warping into ever-more extraordinary new forms, as gospel, country, blues, R&B and more coalesced to create the unstoppable entity known as rock'n'roll.

The tapestry of musical pioneers who laid the groundwork for *Here's Little Richard* – particularly those in the late '40s and early '50s – is vast and complex. It's a ragged patchwork that takes in Jackie Brenston and His Delta Cats' 1951 freak show 'Rocket 88' (reportedly penned by Ike Turner and often dubiously called the first rock'n'roll song) as well as gospel crooners the Clovers, who stitched a rich seam of vulgarity into their smooth tunes. The Washington group's must-hear track, 1954's insolent 'Your Cash Ain't Nothing But Trash', boasts a ribald sax solo that's more 'Tutti Frutti' than the Fruit of the Holy Spirit.

If you were to identify three primary influences that helped to create the King and Queen of Rock'n'roll, though, you'd do well to look at louche R&B don Fats Domino, whose session players recorded much of Richard's debut album at the magical J&M Recording Studio, as well as 1930s pop-gospel pioneer Sister Rosetta Tharpe and the sadly forgotten jump blues joker Louis Jordan. The impact of these seminal artists rests deep in the grooves of *Here's Little Richard*.

In order to really understand the record, then, let's get to know them a little better, shall we?

~

'When you see Elvis Presley singing early songs in his career,' Gayle Wald, the author of *Shout, Sister, Shout! The Untold Story of Rock-and-roll Trailblazer Sister Rosetta Tharpe*, has explained, 'I think [you should] imagine that he is channelling Rosetta Tharpe.' This, Wald noted, goes against the grain of rock music history that's unduly favourable – to put it mildly – towards skinny pale dudes: 'We don't think about the black woman behind the young white man.'

Elvis took inspiration from the so-called Godmother of rock'n'roll's unique, lick-heavy style of guitar picking, which would also influence Chuck Berry. Little Richard, meanwhile, loved her brassy, highly emotional singing style and penchant for raunch (see her scandalous come-on 'I Want a Tall Skinny Papa', which sent gospel purists reeling in 1942).

Sister Rosetta proved an enduring obsession for Richard, who, in the last ten years of his life, implored Tom Jones to perform her signature song 'Strange Things Happening Every Day'. It began when Jones mentioned his grown-up grandchildren: '[Richard] said' – the Welsh crooner slips into a fey, startlingly accurate Little Richard impression – '"*Can they sing? I know they can!*" I said, "Yeah, they can sing." He said, "Now, you've got to form the Tom Jones Gospel Quartet, and here's the song I want you to sing". And he sang "Strange Things Happening Every Day"'. Jones then revealed to Richard that, as it happened, he closed his set with that song every night: 'Well, he went berserk!'

There are great parallels between the life of Little Richard and that of Sister Rosetta Tharpe. She was semi-openly bisexual (and was reportedly in a relationship with fellow gospel singer Marie Knight; together they made the unusual and, in the late '40s, risky move of touring without male accompaniment). And Tharpe found herself attracted to both the spiritual fulfilment of gospel and the thrill and financial reward of something approaching rock'n'roll.

She was born in Cotton Plant, Arkansas, in 1915. At the age of six, she joined her newly divorced mother Katie Bell Nubin on the road as a travelling evangelist for the Church of God in Christ. They headed north to Chicago, flowing in the same direction as Black migrants who brought the blues from the Mississippi Delta and jazz from New Orleans. These influences coalesced at the Roberts Temple Church of God in Christ, where the young Rosetta became the big draw, playing guitar atop the church piano.

When she later shipped out to New York City, Tharpe became a regular at the Cotton Club, an upmarket joint catering to white audiences. In a move that might sound familiar, the 23-year-old swapped spiritual songs for more risqué material that pleased a night-time audience. 'She was criticized and ostracised', Tharpe's friend Roxie Moore said. 'I mean, the church people thought that she had just gone way off.'

Sister Rosetta Tharpe was arguably more successful than Little Richard at balancing her sacred and secular musical lives, performing gospel to Black audiences in church during the daytime and suggestive big band bangers to white audiences in ritzy clubs at night. Listen to her first crossover hit, 'Rock Me', released on Decca Records in 1938, and Tharpe's lusty growl might lead you to suspect she longs for you to do something other than 'rock' her.

The Sister soon became a star, amassing a fortune through her controversial pop tracks and upbeat gospel numbers such as the smoky Southern radio staple 'Two Little Fishes, Five Loaves of Bread'. It was this success that brought Sister Rosetta Tharpe to the Macon City Auditorium, where the young Richard Penniman was flogging Coca-Cola in the years before he wove her soulful suggestiveness and religious fervour into *Here's Little Richard*.

Amazed at seeing his favourite singer on his home turf, he loitered around the venue as the band were setting up, catching Tharpe's attention by singing, naturally, 'Strange Things Happening Every Day'. The superstar was impressed – this story comes via Richard; of course she was – and invited him to perform onstage with her later that night.

'Everybody applauded and cheered and it was the best thing that had ever happened to me', the Georgia Peach recalled. 'Sister Rosetta gave me a handful of money after the show – about thirty-five or forty dollars – and I'd never had so much money in my life.'

~

With his fistful of dollars, Richard was learning where a bit of sexed-up gospel might get you. And he gleaned just as much from Louis Jordan, who was born in Brinkley, Arkansas (little over eleven miles from Sister Rosetta's birthplace) in 1908. The bandleader covered a bizarrely eclectic range of styles, which scored him fifty-four top ten hits between 1942 and 1951 – including a whopping eighteen number ones.

Unbelievably, according to Record Research, Inc., Louis Jordan is *still* the fifth most successful artist on the all-time *Billboard* R&B chart (though the figures were last updated in 2016: back then, says Paul Haney, a researcher at the company, 'Drake was ranked at number six – surely he has surpassed him by now'). Despite his massive contribution to the formation of rock'n'roll, however, Louis has been all but written out of music history. One potential reason is simple racism, the Black maestro wildly underrated just as Little Richard would be. Another is that he shifted between so many different sounds – swing, jump blues, traditional jazz, early rock'n'roll and even proto-rap – that he's slipped through the cracks of genre-led critical analysis. The brother from Brinkley was too rock'n'roll for the jazzers and too jazzy for the rock'n'rollers.

Jordan wasn't the first big band musician, feeling the wartime pinch, to slim his group down to around half a dozen. And he wasn't the first to find that the resultant sound, which came to be known as jump blues, was faster and looser – but none did it with as much panache as he and his Tympany Five. Thanks to his swing, sense of humour and loads – and *loads* – of daft songs about food ('Beans and Cornbread', 'You're My Meat' and simply, erm, 'Onion'), Jordan 'made the blues jump', even if he did say so himself. Not for nothing has he been dubbed 'the Grandfather of Rock'n'roll'. What with Sister Rosetta, that's some unruly family tree.

His crowning glory, the horny bar-room blues belter 'Caldonia', is pretty much a Little Richard song ten years before 'Tutti Frutti', as Jordan rides an undulating piano riff to rhapsodize about a 'long, lean and lanky' hottie. Summoning the spirit of rock'n'roll a full decade ahead of schedule, its most Richard-esque moment arrives when Louis yelps, 'Caldon-IA! Caldon-IA! What make your big head so hard! Mop!'. The song became a smash-hit and was accompanied by a similarly successful short film, helping to make him one of the most sought-after live performers in America.

Sure enough, that ringing refrain caught Richard Penniman's ear. His older cousin, Willie Ruth Howard, told David Kirby that when he was a child, the future rocker would sing Louis Jordan songs and batter out tunes on whatever he could find. Richard himself revealed that he bulldozed through 'Caldonia', the first secular song he ever learned to play, as a means of enticing passers-by to Dr Hudson's Medicine Show in the years before stardom beckoned.

Sadly, Jordan was bafflingly po-faced about the revolution he helped to inspire. In 1960, he gave rock'n'roll 'just about one year more', lamenting: 'The music is bad if the words are good. We started it, but it's been changed.' An uptight and contradictory character – a bigamist and, according to his second wife Ida Fields, a closeted bisexual – he was inherently opposed to the unpredictability of the genre. Pianist Bill Doggett said he 'used to tell [his band], "Don't play anything you can't play twice"'. When his popularity waned as a result of the new sound in the early '50s, he retreated to the comfort of big band leadership, despite that style's parallel decline in popularity. It was commercial suicide.

He didn't even have money to fall back on. Louis' third wife Fleecie Moore collected the royalties he should have made from 'Caldonia' and other hits because, in a publishing ruse gone wrong, he falsely credited her as having written them. (The couple separated in 1947 after she stabbed and nearly killed him in bed for having an affair; they reconciled later in the year even as he underwent plastic surgery on the facial scars she'd inflicted.)

In her 2005 memoir *The Debutante That Went Astray*, though, Louis' fifth and final wife Martha Jordan remembered the former millionaire as happier than he might have been. After all, Decca Records recording director Milt Gabler once admitted that he coached Bill Haley and his Comets, the first of the rock'n'roll acts who succeeded the jump blues shouters, 'to project the way that Jordan's group had done', a debt that Haley never publicly acknowledged. In 1953, after a decade-and-a-half together, Decca declined to renew Louis' contract. The following year, the label released Bill Haley's cover of Big Joe Turner's 'Shake Rattle and Roll', shifting a million copies in the process.

Yet Louis Jordan's influence lives on in *Here's Little Richard*, be it via the cheeky sense of humour that defines 'Slippin' and

Slidin', the comically exaggerated lust of 'She's Got It' or the yelped vocal delivery that punctuates the record. He might have been swept aside by the advent of rock'n'roll, but the greatest album in the genre's history might not exist without him.

In an atypically politicized interview in 1973, Jordan made no bones about what Bill Haley, the pale dude who usurped him, represented: 'As a black artist I'd like to say one thing: there is nothing that the white artist has invented or come along with in the form of jazz or entertainment . . . Rock'n'roll was not a marriage of rhythm and blues and country and western. That's white publicity. Rock'n'roll was just a white imitation, a white adaptation of negro rhythm and blues.'

~

If there's one man whose boogie-woogiefied early R&B completes the blueprint of *Here's Little Richard*, it's glacially paced Louisiana don Fats Domino, whose languid baritone flows like a river of codeine. The pianist shifted more than thirty million records for Imperial between 1955 and 1962 and was, as Arnold Shaw said in *Honkers and Shouters: The Golden Years of Rhythm and Blues*, 'one of the few black artists of the '50s who bridged [R&B and rock'n'roll]'.

Like Richard, Antoine Dominique Domino Jr. played piano in a bouncy, cartoony style. Like Little Richard, too, he had a warm sense of humour – but where our man was manic, Domino was deadpan, with sleepy music to match. The New Orleans native rarely raised so much as an eyebrow and was most at home sat behind the piano, not astride it. That's not to say there was nothing risqué about his act: Domino's debut single, 1949's ironically nimble 'The Fat Man', saw him boast: 'They call me The Fat Man / 'Cause I weigh 200 pounds / All the girls they love me / 'Cause I know my way around.'

This has also been dubbed the first rock'n'roll song; no wonder Elvis crowned him 'the real King' of the genre. Fats made it big after successfully rebranding himself from R&B cat to rock'n'roller in the mid-'50s, but really he was always more comfortable as the former. Unlike the wildmen who followed him, Domino was a shy fellow, which has been attributed to embarrassment at the fact that he never even completed primary school. Or maybe he knew that the secret to being cool is not to look like you're trying: in later years, he refused to leave New Orleans because he didn't like the food anywhere else. He even turned down an offer to perform at the White House in 1998, and the food's probably pretty good there.

Imperial Records founder Lewis Chudd claimed to have discovered Domino in a New Orleans club 'called the Hideaway bar or Dew Drop Inn'. Six years later, of course, the latter became the site of rock'n'roll's Ground Zero when Richard cracked the crows up with his bum sex banger. Fats also cut most of his hits, including 'The Fat Man', at the J&M Recording Studio, where the erstwhile Princess Lavonne detonated pop culture with 'Tutti Frutti' in 1955.

When Domino's backing band brought his groove to that seismic song and throughout *Here's Little Richard*, it's as though they were passing the baton to our subject, who finished what their boss man rolled slowly – very slowly – towards the finish line. But although 'Tutti Frutti' was the first *true* rock'n'roll song, predating Elvis's electrifying take on Big Mama Thornton's 'Hound Dog' by almost a year, the Living Flame could not flicker without the oxygen of the scene around him.

'The '50s was a great time', says Tom Jones, who first heard early American rock'n'roll records in a former army barracks remade as a dancehall in his hometown of Pontypridd, Wales, 'because the music scene changed from big band music into rhythm sections.'

In 1970, the singer asked legendary bandleader Count Basie, who'd found fame in the 1930s, what he made of the disruptive genre:

> He said, 'Well, they just concentrated on the rhythm section. The blues records that old black people used to do, they didn't have any money, so they'd just stick a bloody microphone in the middle of the room and whoever was playing would pick it up.' When you heard 'Rock Around the Clock', which was the first [hit] by Bill Haley and the Comets, it was so hot, he said, because they'd miked each instrument. You know, he broke it down. He said: 'That's the difference: it *sounds* different. It's only twelve-bar blues. When I started, I played stride piano, and it just got bigger.' Music just got bigger.

Jones praises the resourcefulness of pioneering '50s producers who 'made do with what they had' – the likes of Sun Records founder Sam Phillips: 'He didn't have an echo chamber, so he created one with running one tape faster than the other, and it created the "Sun sound". It was a unique echo sound, but he did it out of desperation.'

In fact, Bill Haley, having usurped Louis Jordan, found *himself* pushed from the precipice of history when Phillips's once-in-a-lifetime discovery, some 20-year-old kid from Tupelo, Mississippi, shifted a million copies of a weird tune called 'Heartbreak Hotel', which was issued in January 1956. He was ten years younger than Haley, *much* better-looking and, with his faster, shuffling tempos, happier to break the chains of the swing years that preceded them.

Elvis Presley cut and released his first single, the countrified toe-tapper 'That's All Right', in July 1954. The pill-popping Jerry Lee Lewis rolled up to the Sun Studio in November 1956 to forcefully – and successfully – demand an audition. These touchstones are the before and after of 'Tutti Frutti'. Richard Penniman was by no means the only '50s rock'n'roller to combine pop-gospel, jumps blues and southern R&B, but he is the one who did it the most boldly, queerly and fearlessly, and with absolutely the most at stake.

'I didn't think Elvis was wild', admits Dave Grohl. 'I thought Elvis was, you know' – the rocker reaches carefully for the right words – 'a gorgeous, iconic crooner. And I looked at Little Richard like he was a punk-rock motherfucker. A madman!'

And soon his revolution would need a soundtrack.

'Oooh boy! You better play that thing!'

4
Making it

'I'll tell you', confided Charles Connor in 2009, 'a lot of places we played down South, like Amarillo, Texas, they locked Richard up from shaking his hips on the bandstand. They'd lock him up, stop the concert [and] throw him in jail . . . Richard's manager would have to pay a fine – $150, $200 . . . And they said, "You better not come back here shaking your hips like that – like a crazy man."'

The Upsetters drummer, reflecting on the incident from the *Here's Little Richard* era, recalled the authorities' parting shot: '"And let me tell you something else before you leave: there's another guy coming here. He shakes his hips and everything like you. . . . His name is Elvis Presley, and if you see Elvis Presley, tell him he'd better not bring his redneck behind here, shaking and acting the fool on the stage like coloured people. We gonna lock him up, too."'

To be fair, the King had probably already got the message himself. In the run-up to Elvis's 1956 show in Jacksonville,

Florida, one Judge Marion Gooding prepared arrest warrants for the charge of 'impairing the morals of minors', which he threatened to serve should the star 'put obscenity and vulgarity in front of our children'.

This was part of a moral panic about rock'n'roll itself (epitomized when the White Citizens Council of North Alabama decried the movement for bringing 'people of both races together'). In some ways, then, the Georgia Peach and the boy from Tupelo faced similar opposition in the genre's early days. Yet while Richard endured the additional, incalculable danger presented by the colour of his skin in the Jim Crow era, he also seemed to drive less pearl-clutching horror into the hearts of the nation's press.

After all, Elvis was almost cancelled when he performed a particularly raunchy, hip-thrusting 'Hound Dog' on *The Milton Berle Show* in June 1956. In *The Daily News*, columnist Ben Gross slammed the carry-on as 'the kind of animalism that should be confined to the dives and bordellos'. A few weeks later, the King was forced to atone for the furore by appearing in top-and-tails, crooning the tune to a non-plussed Bassett Hound on the family-friendly *Steve Allen Show*. 'It was', Priscilla Presley said decades later, 'humiliating'.

Aside from the fact that 'Long Tall Sally' was banned by radio stations in Houston, there is no equivalent moment in the story of Little Richard – even though his entire act was far more sexualized, raucous and challenging to the status quo than his rival's. As mega-fan John Waters pointed out: '[With his] outfits and his clothes and his full makeup . . . he was really ahead of his time.'

The cult film-maker noted that Richard's 'girlish' appearance 'really shocked people', but there were no column inches calling for him to be banned. 'Not only was he black', Waters continued, 'not only was he screaming "Lucille" up in your white kid's bedroom – he was practically a drag queen . . . [But] I don't remember anybody being uptight about Little Richard's sexuality during all the '50s. I never heard anything about it. You look at the pictures and think, "I wonder why nobody said anything!"'

The answer, perhaps, is that Richard was so flagrant, so new and so *weird* that the true nature of his transgressions simply did not register in the minds of middle America. Because he wasn't blurring the racial lines in quite the same way as Elvis, he was shocking in the manner of a cartoonish comedian; an entertaining diversion, but not, to the Ben Grosses of the world, worth locking your sons and daughters up over. He slipped into the mainstream because the reality of him was unthinkable.

All of this was by design. The hugely emotionally intelligent Richard Penniman had read the situation instinctively. 'We decided that my image should be crazy and way-out', he said, 'so that the adults would think I was harmless.'

In *American Nightmare: The History of Jim Crow*, author Jerrold M. Packard listed the 'lapses' in 'racial etiquette' for which African-Americans might be assaulted in the segregated South. These, he wrote, included but were not limited to the 'crimes' of 'getting above themselves whether with a too new or too fancy car or a suit of too fine a cut, or – deadliest of all for the transgressor – an inadvertent or casual or misplaced indication of a black man's interest in a white female'.

At the height of his fame, Richard pulled up to venues in Cadillacs, while Charles Connor fondly remembered over-awed female fans assailing the band with 'a shower of panties'; the first time it happened, he boasted, 'I picked a pair up on my stick and waved them in the air.' It's hard to imagine how they could have done much more to provoke the bigots.

In order to avoid trouble, Richard said, he'd lean into his campiness and 'appear in one show dressed as the Queen of England and in the next as the Pope'. Connor, meanwhile, revealed that the band wore 'loud', camp outfits 'in order to play the white clubs, so we wouldn't be a threat to the white girls – so the white audience wouldn't see all those coloured boys digging 'em'.

This was part of the larger-than-life persona that defined Little Richard's wild performances with the Upsetters. 'He was just so animated', Candi Staton says warmly. 'He would get up on top of the piano, he would get one foot on top of the piano, and I'm like, "Oooh boy! You better play that thing!" It was *amazing*, what he did.'

~

Middle America might have missed Little Richard's queerness in the mid-'50s, but Joan Jett, who famously retained the female pronouns in her hit 1981 cover of 'Crimson and Clover', heard it loud and clear. 'It was part of [his] appeal for me', she reflects. 'He was different. I was aware of that side of Richard while I was growing up, learning about rock'n'roll and gender identity. I've come to admire and respect, more and more, Richard's courage, independence and apparent comfort in his own skin.'

The adolescent Richard was so comfortable in his own skin he attempted to regale his mother with tall tales from Macon's queer scene; she stopped this kind of talk in its tracks. Leva Mae was supportive, but the woman had her limits. In those days, Richard would cruise around the city's Greyhound Bus Station, where he'd later claim he wrote some of his greatest tunes, looking for sex 'till three or four in the morning'. On one such night, he said, he met Esquerita, the aspiring R&B musician who would be a big influence on his look and musical direction. It was around this time he also met the flamboyant Billy Wright, an openly gay singer who was known, in his native Atlanta, as 'the Prince of the Blues'.

'Esquerita', explains Billy Vera, 'taught [Richard] to make a piano sound as though he could play it.' Richard, meanwhile, said of Billy Wright, whose persona oozed with sex appeal and sass: 'He really enthused my whole life. I thought he was the most fantastic entertainer I had ever seen.' Billy Wright and Esquerita were both loud, proud, queer performers; the former blathered himself in Pancake 31 make-up and each of them wore stacked pompadours. Both rocked pencil moustaches that would later get a John Waters co-sign. Sound familiar?

Wright even introduced Richard to Zenas Sears, an influential DJ at the Atlanta radio station WGST, who helped the Georgia Peach ink a record deal with RCA Victor. It wasn't much of a contract, mind. The imprint committed to eight limited-run sides, recorded at WGST Studio between October 1951 and January 1952, with Richard entitled to half a cent's worth of royalties on each one he sold – an arrangement that would plague him elsewhere in later years, as we shall see.

The self-penned weepie 'Why Did You Leave Me' and the cut-and-shut jump blues vehicle 'Taxi Blues' did not speak to Richard Penniman's talent. Sears, though, gave airplay to the latter's B-side – 'Every Hour'. Musically, it's a pretty standard blues in the vein of Billy Wright. Vocally, however, it's a tantalizing glimpse of things to come: Richard sounds ripe with sexual longing, his voice catching as he implores: 'I'm crying, "Have mercy – please have mercy on me."'

This is a more passive lyric than those he would later favour (perhaps he didn't yet have the confidence for the tongue-in-cheek naughtiness of 'True Fine Mama', whom Richard would summon to his 'beck and call'), but you can see why 'Every Hour' became the local hit that so pleased his father. Elements of *Here's Little Richard* twinkle through the track, be it the urgent passion that later surfaced on 'Can't Believe You Wanna Leave' or the melodrama of 'Oh Why?'.

~

In March 1957, *NME* recounted how, in the early '50s, Richard began to explore the showbiz world outside of Georgia: 'In Nashville, he met up with three young struggling vocalists whose enthusiasm and lack of ready money equalled his own. . . . With Richard's assistance, a new vocal group – the "Tempo Toppers", with Little Richard as featured vocalist – was born.'

He and the newly minted band embarked on the 'Chitlin' Circuit'. Formed in the 1930s, this was a string of mostly Southern venues, named after an affordable kitchen specialty made from pig intestines, where Black entertainers could perform in relative safety. Since the 1920s, African-American artists' work had been categorized as 'race music' and released on majors' subsidiary labels (Decca Records, for instance, had the 'Sepia Series'). *Billboard* magazine published a 'Race Records' chart – which was entirely separate from the charts that documented the success of white musicians – between 1945 and 1949, when it was rebranded as 'Rhythm and Blues Records'. In the grim Jim Crow years, then, Black artists had their own alternative live ecosystem as well as their own charts.

'You're not an entertainer – especially a black entertainer – if you didn't go through the Chitlin circuit', says Candi Staton. '[It] was a whole different circuit than anything you would ever dream in the music industry.'

The singer followed Little Richard onto this network of characterful clubs in the 1960s. Cheap and cheerful Chitlin' venues were often 'bring your own booze affairs'. Then, as now, this did not always end well. 'People would get too drunk', Staton laughs.

> You got a lot of people screaming at you 'cause they came to hear one song. After they got so many drinks down 'em, they would start acting up – sometimes they had to be put out. There would be fights that would break out in the clubs: you know, somebody's hittin' on somebody's woman and they'd get in a fight and break up the whole

night. Everybody's running and trying to get out of the building! Sometimes they'd pull guns. It was really an interesting period of my life. It was the college of soul music.

Unlike the ghettoized labels, whose Black artists were generally invited to take or leave contracts inferior to those of their white counterparts, Chitlin' venues were Black-owned and the circuit could be celebratory and warm. 'We would go to [certain clubs] so often, everybody was like family', says Staton. 'You'd have people that you just wanted [to visit]: "I'm gonna see so-and-so." Promoters became friends and stuff. The good ones did – the ones that took your money didn't.'

~

It was on the Chitlin' Circuit, in 1953, that Little Richard recruited the Upsetters. The band would earn fifteen dollars each per gig, traversing the South in a station wagon emblazoned with their moniker. At Richard's insistence, his own fee matched theirs. On these tours, they'd cover '40s R&B shouter Roy Brown, Fats Domino and Richard's old pal Billy Wright; the latter's aching 'Keep Your Hands on Your Heart' became a staple of their shows.

Despite the circuit's familial atmosphere, it was obviously difficult for Black entertainers to find a bed for the night during Jim Crow. With typical front, though, Richard claimed this was yet another barrier he overcame. He recalled in 2008: 'I always demanded my way. I had a lot of mouth! And

I would talk and someone would say, "Oh go on, Richard!",
and they'd put me on in the room. And I didn't tell nobody.'

He did admit, elsewhere, that he wasn't *entirely* impervious
to the discrimination of the day, telling *GQ* in 2012: '[I] used
to get beaten up for nothing. [People] slapped in my face
with sticks. The police used to stop me and make me wash
my face. I always tried to not let it bother me. We could stay
in no hotels and go to no toilets. I went to the bathroom
behind a tree. I slept in my car.'

Dave Grohl is in awe of his idol's resilience in the face of
this brutality and prejudice: 'He would hit the road and there
were places where he was just not allowed to be because of
the colour of his skin, and then he'd jump onstage and bring
joy. And so imagine: pushing through that adversity with
the intention of bringing joy to others, when he probably
sacrificed a lot of his own.'

Indeed, because no Little Richard quote could end
without optimism and joy – no matter how appalling the
circumstances – he also told *GQ*: 'I knew there was a better
way and that the King of Kings would show it to me. I was
God's child. I knew God would open that door.'

The Georgia Peach was back in Macon, resting between
tours at the Macon City Auditorium in early 1955, when God
sent him a black-and-gold Cadillac. Out stepped Lloyd Price,
the biblical success of his million-selling 1952 single 'Lawdy
Miss Clawdy' still radiating from every pore. Richard, with
Bud's love of cars and luxuries awakened in his soul, knew
that Price had what he wanted – and *deserved*. He accosted
the singer as he had accosted Sister Rosetta Tharpe, and in

the exact same spot, grabbing onto passing celebrity as if it could deliver him directly to Hollywood.

Price advised the young Richard Penniman to send an audition tape to Specialty Records, the label that released 'Lawdy Miss Clawdy'. And so, in February 1955, he headed to WBML, where he made those scratchy recordings of 'Wonderin'' and 'He's My Star'. He wrapped up the resulting reel of tape in a sheet of dog-eared paper and posted it courtesy of Art Rupe, the man who would change everything.

Little Richard had stumbled upon his big break. *Finally*. But if rock'n'roll and the love of God were two key themes in his life, there was also a third: getting in his own way.

'A cornerstone of R&B, rock'n'roll and gospel'

5
Specialty Records

It was when Richard Penniman was on the cusp of stardom, waiting to hear back about that unsolicited audition tape, which would result in *Here's Little Richard* and prove a railroad switch in the course of modern music history, that the Georgia Peach was arrested at a Macon gas station.

He had been joyriding with a woman who invited men to have sex with her in the car while he watched. After Richard spent a few days in the cooler, his lawyer assured a court that the singer would leave Macon, a price his client accepted as the cost of avoiding further penance for the charge of 'lewd conduct'. The arrest and subsequent banishment from the city must have been painful for an artist who took an endearing amount of civic pride in his hometown, always seeing to it that his interviewers put its name in print (in 1970, blazing the comeback trail, he announced: 'I am the beautiful Little Richard from way down in Macon, Georgia!').

But Little Richard at least had distractions: The Upsetters spent the next ten months honing their act as they ripped it up on the road. Then came the call from Art Rupe, who would become his mentor, saviour and foe – and whose life would forever be defined by the talent he heard in that dog-eared audition tape.

~

Art Rupe founded Specialty Records over a decade before the controlled detonation that was *Here's Little Richard*. Born Arthur Goldberg to a working-class Jewish family in 1917, he grew up in Greensburg, Pennsylvania, where he was exposed to the formations of the music he would later help to amplify.

In 2021, Billy Vera told this writer for *NME*:

> Every Sunday he would go to sit on the kerb in front of the local black church just to listen to the music all day. . . . And he fell in love with that music. In those days, among Jewish people who had been persecuted in every country they've ever been in, they felt a connection to black people who were persecuted in a lot of countries as well. And Art did love black music.

In his early twenties, Art Rupe (as he'd become known after learning that his ancestral family went by that surname in Europe) departed Virginia Polytechnic Institute and Miami University in Oxford, Ohio, taking his vintage Pontiac on a symbolic one-way journey to Hollywood. He took the $2,500 he'd earned as a shipyard engineer and ploughed it into the fledgling independent label Atlas Records. He duly lost most of the money but sold his interest for $600 and, in 1944, went it alone by founding his first original label. 'They had these places called mail-and-desk services that would answer the phone for you', he recalled. 'I'd rent a desk, with a cigar box for my mail, all for two dollars a month.'

This desk became the home of Juke Box Records. Rupe 'went down to a black neighbourhood, [to] black records stores', recounts Vera. 'He said, "I bought $200 worth of records, the good ones and the bad ones" – he's a very methodical man – and said, "I studied these records to determine how I could make records that would sell." And he did a pretty good job of it.' Rupe, his friend explains, timed the songs 'with a stopwatch' to measure the lengths of intros and solos on commercially successful tunes, which were ripe for imitation.

Having spotted that a tantalizing number of recent hits had the word 'boogie' in their titles, the fledgling impresario put out Juke Box's first single. The Sepia Tones' freewheeling – if cynically named – instrumental 'Boogie #1' shifted around 70,000 copies, opening the door to a career holding chamber that Rupe would eventually transcend with the world-shaping Specialty Records. The cash funded three further Juke Box signings, who staked their claims for greatness in 1946: Roosevelt Sykes's suggestive 'Ice Cream Freezer' flopped, but Roy Milton's chirpy 'Milton's Boogie' and Marion Abernathy's buoyant 'Voo-It Voo-It' both reached number four on the *Billboard* chart.

In releasing these records, Rupe overcame the same obstacles that every American label faced in the fallout from the Second World War. Before vinyl became the preferred format in the mid-'50s, shellac was king. During the conflict, though, the US government decreed that the material be redirected to its war effort. Phonograph records accounted for about 30 per cent of the country's shellac consumption, but President Franklin D. Roosevelt oversaw a 70 per cent reduction in their production. A willing public, meanwhile, donated their own shellac discs to be recycled and remade in aid of the conflict.

With the old technology phased out, the record production industry's focus turned to cheaper and lighter vinyl, whose 33 ⅓ (hiya!) revolutions per minute could carry up to forty-five minutes of music; shellac packed in a mere three to five. The die was cast for albums such as *Here's Little Richard* to scoop listeners up on epic sonic journeys.

Before he could make that sensational move, though, Art Rupe had a problem in the short term. Like other shrewd independent record label owners, his initial solution to the 1940s shellac shortage was to scrounge scraps of the material from local suppliers; eventually, he acquired two pressing plants of his own – one in downtown LA and another in Hollywood. 'We pressed only our own records and opened the plants because we couldn't meet the demand of the growing market', Rupe said. 'We were small. We had no more than ten or fifteen presses.'

In doing so, the canny mogul also spotted an opportunity: America's major labels had allowed a blind spot to creep across the record industry. And Art Rupe was intent on manoeuvring into it.

~

The shellac shortage led to cost-cutting measures at major labels. 'Decca, RCA and Columbia were trimming their rosters and only concentrating on their major, big-selling artists', says Billy Vera. 'They were neglecting what were known as "specialty" markets. Whether it was black music, whether it was country and western – whatever it was. Art said: "Essentially I took the crumbs off the table of the major companies." He saw a vacuum that needed to be filled.'

After he founded Specialty Records, named in his typically no-nonsense style, Art Rupe spent a decade building up what Vera has described as 'a cornerstone of R&B, rock'n'roll and gospel'. For all his cynicism, his friend claims, Rupe was not simply out to make a buck with little regard to the quality of his product.

'Art was a highly intelligent man', says Vera. 'He had gone to college, unlike any record business people [at the time], but he had studied marketing.' The historian points to the label's eye-catching white, yellow and black logo, its squidgy lettering vibrating with naughtiness and irreverence.

That pops out across the room. If you were at a party and there was a bunch of records spread out at a table, the Specialty one jumped out at you. I asked [Rupe] about that. He said, 'Well, yeah – my marketing professor in university told me that those three colours were the ones that catch the eye.' So that was contrived.

Until Richard arrived, Lloyd Price was the jewel in Specialty's crown – even if Rupe sensed little promise in the singer's live audition. Price, heartbroken at the prospect of oncoming failure, poured an atavistic kind of pain into his performance, holding back tears while he sang. He soon cheered up when 'Lawdy Miss Clawdy' became the top-selling R&B tune of 1952.

The label's roster in this period included Sam Cooke, who was then a moderately successful gospel singer fronting the Soul Stirrers. Rupe also signed a string of little-remembered gospel acts epitomized by Wynona Carr; to her chagrin, he renamed her *Sister* Wynona Carr in an ill-fated bid to recreate the success of Sister Rosetta Tharpe. 'They had a tremendous gospel catalogue', asserts Vera. 'I don't think anybody made better gospel records than Specialty.'

This is telling. For all their differences in temperament and background, Rupe and Richard had much in common – and not least a deep, shared appreciation of the music of the church. When the label boss *finally* listened to the superstar-in-waiting's ratty audition tape, he recognized a soul that spoke the same language as his. 'There was something in his voice I liked', Rupe remembered. 'It was so exaggerated, so over-emotional – and so I said, "Let's give this guy a chance."'

When he was grinding through the Chitlin' Circuit with the Tempo Toppers, Richard had signed a contract with the small-fry Peacock Records. It was just as dire as the RCA Victor one, with the added misery that head honcho Don

Robey was a tyrant who beat Richard for insubordination and would wave a .45 calibre revolver in the faces of artists he deemed disrespectful. In a sign that his intellect was vastly dwarfed by his ego, Robey sold Art Rupe the contract to the greatest rock'n'roll star of all time for just $600.

The Specialty boss, in contrast, made up for lost time when he sent Bumps Blackwell to meet Richard at J&M Recording Studio in September 1955. Little Richard and Art Rupe were two sides of the same coin. The former was too untamed to succeed alone, while the latter's strengths – his clinical and methodical nature, along with his steely and taciturn persona – meant little without a superstar for him to mould. Richard needed a set of parameters for his outrageousness to bounce against; Rupe needed a mercurial talent to breathe life into the empire he had built. Together they created some of the most wild and uninhibited yet perfectly pitched and calibrated music the world has ever heard.

And of course it all ended in tears.

~

The rot set in early. Buoyed by the success of 'Tutti Frutti', Richard – who'd been overawed in the studio a couple of months earlier – swaggered into Hollywood's Radio Recorders for the 29 November follow-up session, which resulted in an early version of 'Long Tall Sally'. This time he insisted he knew better than Rupe, demanding to be backed by a ragged band of New Orleans musicians he had amassed, rather than J&M's crack team of in-house legends. 'I'm not in the habit of paying for a second session on a song', griped a put-out Rupe, 'but this one needed to be done over. It was too slow, and Richard's band just wasn't cutting it.'

If that was a hairline crack, the real structural damage to their relationship was already underway; Little Richard resented the size of the cheques he received from Art. In the mid-'50s, an artist might receive approximately four cents on each record sold at the standard price of eighty-nine cents. The King and Queen of Rock'n'roll took home just *half* a cent per single – exactly the same arrangement that had blighted him at RCA Victor. 'You had to sell two records to make a penny!' he once despaired.

Billy Vera, though, denies there was any funny business when it came to Specialty. 'I've seen the company records', he says. '[Rupe] was not screwing him.'

In 1984, Richard alleged that the businessman had been able to charge himself that rock-bottom rate because he owned Venice Music, the publishing company to which Specialty's songs were licensed. 'See, that's the kind of thing [Richard] wouldn't understand', contests Vera. 'The normal thing [was that] the federal statutory rate [for a song] was two cents. Half to the publisher; half to the writer or writers. So it would be a penny to the publishers, a penny to the writers.'

Richard, remember, didn't write biggest records alone – and often not at all. It's undeniable, though, that Art Rupe was a white man who effectively owned a Black record label. 'Most of the artists back in that era, the black artists, did not get paid right', the Southern Child lamented in 1998. 'Most of these artists was trying to help their families, and they was taken, they was misrepresented, had terrible contracts.'

Vera insists his friend didn't exploit Black artists, citing 'excellent businessman' Lloyd Price's testimony to his scrupulous financial ethics: 'He told me, "As long as Art Rupe owned Specialty Records, I received a statement and a nice, fat cheque for 'Lawdy Miss Clawdy' every six months like clockwork."'

The historian also points to Herald Attractions, the booking agency Rupe formed to promote his gospel artists. It was – and remains – industry standard for an agent to charge around 10 per cent on each show booked through their agency: '[But] he didn't take any money for it. He said, "I just wanted to make sure they were paid properly for it." I mean, who would do that?'

~

After Richard handed his resignation to rock'n'roll, the businessman – with typical abruptness and pragmatism – shut down his epochal record label in 1959. He'd experienced a serious knock after rejecting Sam Cooke's attempts to go pop, inviting him to release the dreamy 'You Send Me', which the singer had written himself, via another label. In doing so, Rupe released Cooke from his Specialty contract. A series of major Hollywood labels turned the song down before the singer teamed up with John and Alex Siamas, a couple of chancers with no experience in the music business – the former specialized in manufacturing plane parts.

'You Send Me', inevitably, reached number one on both *Billboard*'s R&B and pop charts, supersizing Cooke's career in the process. Years later, Art Rupe admitted to Billy Vera: 'Letting Sam go was the biggest mistake I ever made.'

Without a second artist to rival Richard's success and disgusted by the prevalence of payola (whereby labels secretly paid DJs for radio play), he turned his methodical nature natural to the oil industry, amassing a fortune with a lot less hassle. He later opened the charitable Arthur N. Rupe Foundation and, at over a hundred years old, living in Santa Barbara, continued to work in the office five days a week.

Billy Vera last saw his friend in the flesh before the Covid-19 pandemic struck in 2020, when the mogul was '101 or 102' and still 'sharp as a tack'. Asked in March 2021 what kind of person Art Rupe was, Vera replied: 'A very bright man. Very business-like, but with me there's a warmth.'

In that interview, the historian explained: 'He lives alone, although he's got a helper. . . . His memory was always very good [but] he's finally – at 104 – I'm starting . . . I'm catching things that he doesn't remember. And he was never like that. It's not often, but it's the minor details.' This deterioration, Vera noted, coincided with 'being stuck in the house' due to pandemic-induced self-isolation.

Art Rupe died less than a month after that conversation was taped.

For the fourteen years in which he ran Specialty Records, and for many decades beyond that, the mastermind who recorded and compiled *Here's Little Richard* was a force of nature (even if his style of business attracted controversy). When others saw a flailing R&B singer, or even a 'sissy', Art Rupe saw immeasurable spirit and potential, a tornado of talent that could realign the boundaries of pop music forever.

In many ways, he was a kind of pseudo father figure to our subject – who, along with the other musicians at J&M, referred to him by the nickname 'Pappy' – even if their relationship wasn't much less complicated than Richard and Bud's. Given that he conceived and oversaw *Here's Little Richard* down to the smallest details, Rupe arguably shares authorship of the record, which would prove to be the totem of their enduring legacy.

But first he needed to embed his superstar in the public consciousness – and here the mogul had another ace card to play.

Figure 5.1 'Here's – Little Richard!': The *New Musical Express* heralds our hero's arrival in March 1957. Courtesy of NME Networks.

Figure 5.2 'He's never made a record that wasn't a hit!': The *New Musical Express* tells the 'truth' about Little Richard in September 1957. Courtesy of NME Networks.

'Beyond glamour'

6
The Girl Can't Help It

A young boy wolf-whistles. A sizzling blonde swaggers down the street, a block of ice melts in her wake and – most suggestively of all – a milkman clutches a bottle of the white stuff that bubbles up and spurts all over his fist as she swishes by. The scene could only be soundtracked by Little Richard, who bellows through the movie's raunchy title track: 'If she winks an eye, the bread slice turns to toast / She got a lot of what they call "the most"!'

At Art Rupe's behest, Little Richard came crashing into the mainstream with *The Girl Can't Help It*. Released in 1956, the film did for Richard and rock'n'roll what the 'Smells Like Teen Spirit' music video would later do for Nirvana and '90s grunge, crystalizing his musical persona while sending the scene he epitomized overground. Where Kurt Cobain stared down the camera through tangled blonde hair, exuding the apathy and boredom that came to define Gen X, our man stood defiantly up at the piano in a cartoonishly oversized grey suit, encompassing the good-natured rebelliousness of the 1950s.

He doesn't act in the film, instead rocking out onstage in a key scene, but Richard is certainly one of its stars. The story centres on sadsack publicist Tom Miller (Tom Ewell), who was once blessed with a gift for unearthing new talent. Broken-hearted by a former client, the real-life torch singer Julie London (who plays herself), he's turned his talents to sniffing out his next drink instead. That's until small-time gangster "Fats" Murdoch (Edmond O'Brien) enlists him to promote the uber-glamorous Jerri Jordan (Jayne Mansfield) as a singer. The only hitch is that she can't carry a note – though, in-keeping with the movie's satirical nudge, this is less of a hindrance than you'd think in the fickle, newfangled world of rock'n'roll.

The Girl Can't Help It, which also features a host of other performances from other '50s rockers and R&B stars, sees the Georgia Peach roar through the *Here's Little Richard* tracks 'Ready Teddy' and 'She's Got It'. The film introduced a generation of fans to his majestic music. 'I've always liked Little Richard from *The Girl Can't Help It*', says Tom Jones. 'It was tremendous.' Elton John, meanwhile, explains: 'One of my favourite [of his] songs was "The Girl Can't Help It". My mum hated it. She said: *"That bloody row! Little Richard! I don't like him!"* But the film, obviously, with Jayne Mansfield . . . the film is fantastic as well.'

John Waters even paid homage to the camp classic's most famous scene with his 1972 bad taste breakthrough *Pink Flamingos*. Where the original saw Mansfield sashay down the street, melting hearts along with that block of ice, Waters had the drag queen Divine stomp through Baltimore while real-life passers-by looked on agog and Little Richard squalled through 'The Girl Can't Help It' on the soundtrack.

As the ever-direct film-maker said of the scene that inspired him: 'The best entire thing in the movie is when the ice melts and milk bottle pops. Which was really rude for the '50s! I mean, that's very much a cum shot!'

~

The Girl Can't Help It was made for $1,310,000 and went on to gross a whopping $6,250,000. Both were pretty respectable for a rock'n'roll movie back in 1956: the Bill Haley-starring *Rock Around the Clock*, released ten months earlier, was scraped together for $300,000 and did well to have raked back $1.1 million by January 1957.

At this time, the so-called rocksploitation genre was defined by flicks starring Alan Freed, the American DJ widely credited with introducing white audiences to Black artists and pioneering the magical portmanteau 'rock'n'roll'. The Freed vehicles *Don't Knock the Rock* and *Mister Rock and Roll*, both featuring Little Richard and released in 1956 and 1957 respectively, offered young audiences the chance to see their favourite rockers perform in the years before music videos. The films resonated with British fans, too, as out-of-reach American rock stars rarely toured the UK. They were not, however, cult classics.

'Unlike all the other rock'n'roll movies', says Billy Vera, '*The Girl Can't Help It* had a real script, real actors. It was well-filmed and well-directed.' He adds: 'Prior to that, [Richard] had been in a couple of crummy, black-and-white, cheesy, cheap pictures: those two Alan Freed movies were terrible movies. I mean, the kids didn't care – we just wanted to see our rock'n'roll stars.'

John Waters concurred. 'There were a lot of rock'n'roll movies then', he said, 'but this was the Hollywood one – this was the big-time one.'

The Girl Can't Help It was filmed in Deluxe, a garish and short-lived alternative to Technicolor. It's hallucinatory and cartoony – director Frank Tashlin is perhaps best remembered for his work on the *Looney Tunes* animations. The opening credits sequence, in which brightly clothed guys and gals jitterbug around a rainbow-hued sound stage, is so trippily vivid it brings to mind the psychedelic colour treatment on Peter Jackson's 2021 Beatles documentary *Get Back*.

This is not the only way in which Tashlin's film pushed the needle on the rock'n'roll movie. Blues icon B. B. King described *The Girl Can't Help It* as the first film 'that was accepted as an A1 movie featuring blacks', adding: 'It had Fats Domino, Little Richard and several other blacks and presented them in beautiful way. I mean with a lot of class.' Paul McCartney, who first saw the flick as a 14-year-old in Liverpool, similarly said: 'It's still *the* great music film. They had only treated music films as B-pictures up 'til then . . . [like] those little black-and-white productions with Alan Freed as the personality, and lots of what they thought were "black acts". . . . We idolised these people and always thought they were given crummy treatment – until *The Girl Can't Help It.*'

Tashlin's contribution to the rock'n'roll canon also includes a livewire turn from Gene Vincent, the Virginia rockabilly star portentously dubbed the 'Screaming End'. He and his band the Blue Caps' seething rendition of 'Be-Bop-a-Lula', which takes place in a rehearsal space improbably adorned with gold-framed oil paintings, sums up the era's civilization-destroying spirit.

Vincent, noted John Waters, was 'scarier than Elvis' in this scene, which evoked the moral panic around rock'n'roll and fears of juvenile delinquency. 'This was beyond Elvis!' he added. 'Worse! But to put it so slick in this Hollywood lighting and everything? That's what made it cartoonish and almost freakish.'

Billy Vera likewise states: '[Vincent] looks a like a wildman in there. And they do this moment where they scream – "*Aaaargh!*" – and their hats fly off. It's *insane*. It's wonderful. To me, that is one of the quintessential rock'n'roll moments, visually, right up there, almost, with Elvis.'

~

Elvis Presley was, in fact, almost the star of *The Girl Can't Help It*. Keen to have the King in quintessential rock'n'roll movie, the suits at 20th Century Fox approached his formidable manager Colonel Tom Parker, who demanded $50,000 for two songs. When the studio's Head of Production Buddy Adler demurred, the cunning colonel suggested they flip a coin: if Adler won, Elvis would perform *three* songs free of charge; if the Colonel won, the price rose to $100,000. The studio boss demurred again.

Luckily, Little Richard had a scheming pop mastermind in his corner, too. Art Rupe had heard that Fats Domino was lined up to perform the film's title track and campaigned for the studio to reconsider. 'Rupe did a great sales pitch', says Billy Vera. 'He said, "My artist is a lot more exciting visually – you know, Fats just sits there and sings and smiles. Little Richard is more physical – he'll put on a show for ya! The film will capture him in all his excitement." He talked him into it.'

Rupe, who was usually exacting in pursuing his personal vision at studio sessions, approached 'The Girl Can't Help It' as if creating a product for a client. 'I knew the effect I wanted', he said of the song, which had already been composed by singer-songwriter Bobby Troup, 'because the music director at 20th Century Fox told us how they wanted it. . . . Our job was to get a good musical reproduction and make suggestions.'

The track was laid down at J&M Recording Studio in the middle of October 1956, with its fulsome backing vocals provided by Californian doo-woppers the Robins and released as a single that December – though it didn't make the cut for *Here's Little Richard*. Instead, the song appeared on the album's self-titled follow-up in July 1958. The helplessly randy 'She's Got It', meanwhile, was a retooling of 'I Got It', which had been recorded at J&M in February 1956.

The original, a Richard composition, harked back to his early days in Macon when he'd marvel at a vegetable seller who sang about the goods he flogged around the city: 'You can see him every day goin' up and down the street / Always hollerin' 'bout somethin' good to eat.' Rupe enlisted the Italian-American songwriter John Marascalco, who also co-wrote 'Ready Teddy' among other Little Richard tunes, to make it less . . . weird. So that 'little old man with a billy-goat cart' became the more relatable 'sweet little girl that lives down the street'.

Richard cuts a louche figure, standing up at the piano in the centre of a bougie nightclub, when he belts out the song in *The Girl Can't Help It*. Tucked away in a booth, Tom Miller informs Jerri Jordan of his plans for her career 'build-up'. His grand scheme, gleaned from years of experience as an industry strategist at the height of his powers, is to have Jordan parade herself – and her sparkly red dress – around the venue's bedazzled owner on the off-chance of a booking. *Genius*. As she sashays her way through the club, Richard cries in the song's lyrics: 'Ruby lips! Shapely hips! / When she walks by, all the cats flip!'

The scene could seem creepy or even exploitative but is too camp, tongue-in-cheek and ultimately innocent for those definitions. 'Jayne Mansfield has always looked a little like a drag queen', said John Waters, 'but no drag queen can pull it off like Jayne, really, because she's in on [the joke]. That's the thing that makes it so endearing. . . . She sums up the '50s. . . . Nobody's more extreme than Jayne Mansfield in representing a '50s glamour girl gone berserk, really. Beyond glamour! Like, nuts! On acid!'

~

The quintessential rock'n'roll movie? Have you not *seen* Elvis shaking his moneymaker through the world's least secure prison in that iconic dance sequence from *Jailhouse Rock*? In fact, that film, directed by Richard Thorpe, was released almost a year after *The Girl Can't Help It* – and seems to bear some influence of the earlier movie. In Tashlin's flick, Fats Murdoch performs 'Rock Around the Rockpile', an ode to imprisonment he wrote in the slammer, backed by a band decked out in prison stripes. When Elvis belts out the title track in Thorpe's film, he does so in very similar circumstances and with era-defining results.

The legacy of Tashlin's tale doesn't end there: when Paul McCartney successfully auditioned for John Lennon's pre-Beatles band the Quarrymen at Liverpool's St Peter's Church Hall in July 1957, he shuffled his way through 'Twenty Flight Rock', precisely as he'd seen a similarly bequiffed Eddie Cochran do in *The Girl Can't Help It*. (He also played the slinky 'Be-Bop-a-Lula' and wowed Lennon by whooping through a medley of Little Richard songs.) The movie remained a Fab Four favourite in later years, too: in 1968, they rescheduled a studio session for 'The White Album' track 'Birthday' just so that they could watch its British TV premiere instead.

For all its famous fans, though, Frank Tashlin's garish flick has become a cult concern at best. At worst, it's been pretty much forgotten. John Waters and his queer creative cohorts might have coveted the film ('It was something we all watched every year', he said, 'you know – like families watch *The Wizard of Oz*') but, at the time of writing, you can't even legitimately stream *The Girl Can't Help It*. You never hear the movie spoken about in the same breath as other '50s counterculture classics – such as, say, *Rebel Without a Cause*, which was shot on a similar budget and actually took in less at the box office.

Yet the Little Richard vehicle truly captured a moment. 'It was huge', says Billy Vera, who saw the movie, upon its release, at New York's 6,000-capacity Roxy Theatre, which was packed with teenagers. 'It really made [rock'n'roll] more mainstream.' When he fought for his brightest star's appearance in the film, could Art Rupe have known what a big deal it would be? 'Absolutely', insists Vera. 'He knew how important this was to Richard's career.'

The Girl Can't Help It is emblematic of the *Here's Little Richard* era, snapshotting the youthquake that rock'n'roll represented while rightfully casting the Architect as nothing less than iconic. Standing up at that piano with his pompadour preened to perfection, his skin shimmering, Richard 'never looked more beautiful', said John Waters. How typically contrary, then, that, just over ten months after the film first hit cinemas, its breakout superstar would turn his back on the culture he gave birth to in the first place.

'I couldn't swing and I couldn't sway, so I rocked!'

7
Here's Little Richard

After the success of *The Girl Can't Help It*, the stage was set for Little Richard's definitive musical statement, which landed on our planet just three months later. There is no more perfect distillation of the transcendental power of rock'n'roll than *Here's Little Richard*. If you were to effectively crystalize an entire decade's worth of desire, adolescent rebellion, state-sanctioned pain and subversive happiness into under thirty minutes of bass, guitar, drums, sax and vocals, it would sound a lot like this timeless record.

From the opening rallying cry of 'Tutti Frutti' to the closing cacophony of 'She's Got It', this is the sound of a man who appears not only to not give a fuck about contemporary societal norms, but who apparently has no idea they even existed in the first place. There is a sweetness to the record. It's not a rebellion fraught with a sense of danger, anger or even confrontation. In fact, although the album is totemic of a revolution, you may, when the needle hits the groove, feel that Richard Penniman was not consciously resisting the status quo at all. Instead, it seems, he was simply being his Black, queer, effeminate self, channelling the massive capacity for love in his enormous heart.

As we know, though, Richard *did* experience hardship, prejudice and pain for the crime of being himself – be it within his childhood home or on the road with the Upsetters. What's amazing about *Here's Little Richard* is the way in which he seems to rise above other people's squalor to emit only joy. This is not to say that he lacked agency, and he was clearly outspoken (a stunning quote from 1984: 'The Billboard Hot 100 is like a Ku Klux Klan meeting'). But the Originator sounds totally untouchable on this collection of songs, as if he's way, way, *way* higher than the barriers he faced.

After he accidentally kicked off *Here's Little Richard* with the fateful 'Tutti Frutti' session in September 1955, the Living Flame continued to record the bangers that make up the album until he cut 'Jenny, Jenny' at J&M Recording Studio on 15 October 1956. By the time Specialty Records released his LP on 4 March 1957, the following songs had already broken the top ten in the *Billboard* R&B chart: 'Tutti Frutti', 'Long Tall Sally', 'Slippin' and Slidin'', 'Ready Teddy', 'Rip It Up' and 'She's Got It'. To drum up interest in their new context ahead of the album's release, Art Rupe took out a tantalizing ad in *Billboard*: 'Now six of Little Richard's hits and six brand new songs of hit calibre are available in a great LP.'

The wildly productive 'Jenny, Jenny' session that rounded off this studio magic has gone down in history: the group turned out no less than six hit singles, including 'The Girl Can't Help It', in just two days. In the liner notes of 1989's legendary 'Specialty Sessions' boxset from Ace Records, writer Rick Coleman asserted: 'The likes of that session will never be heard again.'

This is emblematic of Richard in his prime, his idiosyncratic style a jolt for the rotating cast of musicians who backed him at these sessions. 'We didn't realize we was creating something different', he told Baton Rouge newspaper *The Advocate* in 1998, 'because they hadn't heard anyone play piano in the style that I was playing. It was kinda different. They were used to recording Fats Domino and Guitar Slim and other people. And thank God we had something different.'

Seeming to refer to himself by the *royal we*, the Quasar concluded: 'That's the reason we're the Architect of Rock'n'roll.'

~

All but three of the tracks on *Here's Little Richard* were laid down at J&M Recording Studio, with the exceptions being 'Baby', 'True, Fine Mama' and 'She's Got It', which were cut in Los Angeles. When David Kirby referred to the 'handmade world' of 'old, weird America' that Penniman lived in, he perfectly summed up J&M, the frankly unimposing space owned by the pioneering engineer Cosimo Matassa.

This sixteen-by-eighteen-foot box lurked at the back of his family's furniture store, where they also flogged fridges and waffle irons. Forget the splendour of, say, London's

Abbey Road Studios, which is vast enough to accommodate a 100-piece orchestra: Bumps Blackwell described Matassa's joint as looking 'like an ordinary motel room'. Even the owner admitted that the set-up amounted to 'three mics and some juggling'. He insisted, though, that there was little precedent for what he was trying to achieve: 'We learned as we went. New Orleans wasn't exactly a pillar of technology. There wasn't any place I could go to somebody else's studio and learn something. . . . It forced me to learn how to do it well.'

There was a small control room adjoined to the performance space. This nerve centre consisted of a suitcase-sized mixing board with four knobs – one for each mic and another to adjust the volume of a track – and a rudimentary Ampex Model 300 tape machine. Luckily, the producer wasn't looking for 'slick'. 'Some of the mistakes that were made', says Kelly Lee Blackwell, 'or what people would consider mistakes, was really what Bumps wanted when he got with Richard doing "Tutti Frutti" and "Long Tall Sally" and "Rip It Up" and "Ready Teddy". I just think he saw mistakes as perfection.'

Blackwell and Matassa's 'juggling' act saw them manoeuvre musicians around the studio to attain the best sound possible in the circumstances. It wasn't simply a case of putting people and instruments together and hitting 'record'; a horn might cut through everything or the drums overpower the rest of the band, submerging the greatest vocalist of all time. So Lee Allen and Alvin 'Red' Tyler blared their saxophones into the keys of a propped-open grand piano to amplify the sound, with a bassist placed at the far end of the room to prevent the sounds from bleeding. Percussionist Earl Palmer found himself sitting just outside the studio with only his drum kit and a second mic for company while Little Richard bellowed his cosmic nonsense into Cosimo Matassa's third and final microphone.

Upon arranging the mics and players in the performance space, Blackwell would return to the next room and check the levels. If they weren't right – and they often weren't – he would need to rearrange them, using only his ear and instinct for guidance. He might spend an hour meticulously arranging the sound levels in that room but, he once recalled, 'When we got it, we got it.' The producer added with pride: 'Once those guys hit a groove, you could go on all night'.

Art Rupe was similarly effusive about Matassa's session men. 'Richard owes his career in large measure to the fact that we had those musicians', he said. 'Those musicians were the best in the world. And, as a matter of fact, rightfully they should have been part of the songwriters' credits, because it was their head arrangements, their imagination and creativity which made our records the success they were.'

All these years later, Tom Jones remains in awe of the New Orleans scene that produced these maestros-for-hire. The city, he says, 'was where all the great piano players come from', adding: 'You know, rock'n'roll, boogie-woogie – that was it.' Still, only one musician was so essential that his presence was required at every session, be it New Orleans or Los Angeles, and that was Richard himself. Jones reveals: 'I said [to him], "How come you sounded so different? And you played so different?" And he said, "When I was young, a man used to come on the radio, *Swing and Sway with Sammy*

Kaye. I couldn't swing and I couldn't sway, so I rocked!" And that was it.'

Where modern musicians make use of imperfection-erasing software, Blackwell would sift through 'sixty or seventy' takes of the band playing a song 'from beginning to end'. Instead of recording various instruments separately and combining them on the finished song – overdubbing – as would become commonplace in the 1960s, he recorded everything to one track: 'Maybe we might go to surgery and intercut a track or cut a track at the end or something, but we didn't know what overdubbing was.'

So, Blackwell said, the 'tracks you heard were the tracks as they were recorded'. Despite having been made in such a spit-and-sawdust manner, *Here's Little Richard* still sounds explosive today – a testament to the talent and ingenuity of the musicians at the helm. 'Handmade' records, though, were all Richard and his co-conspirators knew.

Even when he worked with Elton John on 'The Power' almost forty years later, the Georgia Peach was yet to get familiar with overdubbing. 'It was so extraordinary', says Elton. 'When we sang, he didn't know about dropping in. He didn't realise you could do something and then come back and do it again 'cause he was used to doing it all in one go.'

Recording with Little Richard was an amazing experience that left a lasting impression on Elton John, a superstar who's had no shortage of amazing experiences: 'To be able to make a record with my idol, it's one of the most fabulous things I've ever done.'

~

It was no easy feat to get the Living Flame behind the mic in the first place. 'If it hadn't been for Bumps getting Richard to the studio regularly, we may not have had a Little Richard', Art Rupe asserted. The mercurial singer failed to turn up to some sessions – including a date at J&M in June 1956 – but almost always delivered the goods when Bumps Blackwell was behind the mixing desk.

Cosimo Matassa, who passed away in 2014, once told Kelly Lee Blackwell about her father's special working relationship with Little Richard:

> He said, 'In a recording session with Richard, your dad was dealing with the biggest ego in rock'n'roll . . . I've never come across a man who could do someone like that: he never made Richard feel small and would always allow him to be the star. He knew how to correct him, give him constructive criticism and teach him things and be better. But he never embarrassed him, never belittled him – always allowed him to be Richard. Your father just had a great talent for doing that with him. You could tell that there was a really good bond between them.'

Blackwell started out a bandleader in a jazz ensemble that featured Ray Charles and Quincy Jones before they found fame. He came into Art Rupe's orbit in the early '50s and had an innate appreciation of the burgeoning rock'n'roll movement. 'Daddy could see the future of what this particular style of music was going to do', says Kelly Lee. 'He knew: "I wanna keep putting this kind of music out – this sound, this beat – because I know it's going to have an impact on the music industry and the way people hear music, think about music, *feel* about music."'

Although his roots were in jazz, she adds, 'It turned for him because he was like, "I know this it's going to be a timeless thing; it's going to be classic."'

This is impressive considering that, in the mid-'50s, so many grown-ups and cultural commentators considered rock'n'roll to be a passing fad. Yet, says Kelly Lee, both Richard and Blackwell 'knew they were gonna make history'. Their bond went deep: 'It was more of a father-son type relationship goin' on with them. At my Dad's funeral, Richard gave the eulogy and he always referred to him as "Daddy Bumps". My Dad was a nurturer to Richard – and to other people too.'

Richard was still a teenager when Bud threw him out of the family home for his sexuality. This was, perhaps, a wound that could never truly heal, given the violent nature of the patriarch's death – which occurred when Richard was only nineteen – and the fact that the case was never resolved. And so the young singer found *two* stand-in dads. Blackwell seems to have provided him with a greater sense of safety than Art Rupe, as he later became the King and Queen's manager. They were still collaborating musically in 1973, when they recorded *Right Now!*, their final album together.

'The way my Dad conducted himself with Richard [was] by teaching him', explains Kelly Lee. 'Maybe Richard [thought], "I wish my father would have done it" or "I wish I would have had this opportunity with my father." Someone who's older than you, who's more seasoned, can guide you and lead you.' She adds with a laugh: 'I mean, they butted heads, too. But it's supposed to be that way.'

Although Blackwell could be laissez-faire in the studio, he was also a taskmaster, as those 'sixty or seventy takes' suggest. Of her father's instinct for a song, Kelly Lee says: 'Sometimes you can hear how a song just falls off at the end, and they kept it that way, because that's just the way that it was supposed to flow.' On other occasions, though, 'he would be like, "No, I want it better than this." That's just how he and Richard were together.'

Continuing his lifelong mentorship, Bumps pulled strings to arrange Richard's cameo in the 1986 comedy *Down and Out in Beverley Hills*, which bolstered the Georgia Peach's final comeback to the mainstream. Sadly, the producer died from pneumonia the year before the film was released.

'Daddy was really humble with his music', says Kelly Lee.

He wasn't in it for the money or anything, or the credit – even though I'm really doing my best to get him all the credit he deserves. 'Cause he's just so deserving of it. When I do [interviews], it's like a love letter to him and his incredible legacy. He was just really the kind of person of: 'I just want to put music out. I want people to dance and I want people to sing.'

~

The less humble Richard was up against it in the studio, since his *other* dad was also relentless in his quest for the 'correct' take of a track. Remember that Bumps was working to please the ever-precise Rupe, who would leave detailed 'blueprints' – as the mogul called them – outlining his expectations of a session.

Upon Rupe's insistence, the exhausted musicians revisited tunes across different sessions *ad naseum*. The band would groan when the singer and producer announced, 'One more for Pappy', which became a tongue-in-cheek catchphrase at J&M. The result, though, was that even the previously unheard songs on *Here's Little Richard*, including orphans not deemed worthy of the singles market, shine so brightly it's scarcely believable they weren't rush-released in the first place.

Most artists would *kill* for a 'Baby', an 'Oh Why?' or a 'True, Fine Mama'. However, these album tracks do lean further into R&B than the A-sides that smashed the *Billboard* pop charts. Compare the woozy 'Oh Why?' to the breakneck 'Long Tall Sally' and 'Rip It Up' (which are, tellingly, Joan Jett's joint favourite Little Richard songs). It's perhaps easier to forgive the slowies' original shelving in the context of Specialty's mission to record lightning-quick hits that would capture the rock'n'roll zeitgeist.

Recontextualized by *Here's Little Richard*, the bluesier tunes break up the tracklist to create a sense of pace and rhythm. Here was another of Art Rupe's masterstrokes, and it's to be applauded that he had such a firm grasp on the album as a concept, given that the format was still in its infancy. Elvis might have released two albums by March 1957, while Fats Domino had four to his name, but LPs would not outsell singles until 1968. The businessman was ahead of his time and Chuck Berry, Jerry Lee Lewis and Buddy Holly all followed suit by releasing albums in the wake of Richard's debut. This was Rupe's art.

He was typically pragmatic about the move. 'Richard was such a visual performer', says Billy Vera, 'and [Rupe] wanted to get into the album market. [He] thought a cover with a wild photo of him might grab the teenagers.'

So the label founder enlisted the services of the photography company Globe, whose snapper, explains Vera, shot Richard 'in session, onstage and backstage'. The chosen image, which depicts the sweat-streaked star hollerin' out a crazed war cry even as his shirt remains buttoned up and his collar pin respectfully in place, 'just jumped out'. From there, art directors Thadd Roark and Paul Hartley created the final design: Richard in chaste sepia, the background pop art-orange. It's an image of contrasts: composure and chaos, tradition and futurism. A wrecking ball with a firm hand at the wheel.

The quality of the design, in Vera's mind, set Specialty Records apart from the competition: 'This is really first-class artwork. This is not some piece of crap. The Fats Domino albums, the music was great, but the covers were not on this level.'

You'd be hard-pushed to argue that the cover of Elvis's self-titled debut, which captures the King slammin' on a beat-up guitar, his head thrown back mid-song – the kind of image you *hear* rather than *see* – is not absolutely iconic too. But where Elvis embodies the promise of the '50s, of a better and freer life that needn't look like your parents', there is an alien quality in the artwork of *Here's Little Richard*. Unlike Elvis, he is not in a club with a compadre plugging a bass and revellers in the background. Instead, he is alone. There is an unreality to the way in which he superimposed on that orange backdrop: he looks like he's been similarly beamed onto our planet, always ready to return to his own.

All of this would mean less if the music itself didn't also exude otherworldliness – but Richard even opens the album with his own alien greeting: *Wop-bop-aloo-bop-alop-bom-bom!* The American record-buying public, so unattuned to the concept of the rock album, responded by sending this one to number thirteen on the *Billboard* chart.

'Just keep that steady rhythm'

8
The songs

David Bowie's countercultural awakening began around late 1955, when his father gifted him a grab bag of singles by the likes of Chuck Berry and Fats Domino. 'Then', Bowie recalled, 'I hit gold: "Tutti Frutti" by Little Richard – my heart nearly burst with excitement. I'd never heard anything even resembling this. It filled the room with energy and colour and outrageous defiance. I had heard God.'

Curiously, though – and at the risk of committing blasphemy – the spectacular 'Tutti Frutti' doesn't quite move like the rest of the rockers on *Here's Little Richard*. Separate it from the seismic vocal of its main attraction, and the song shimmies at a slightly more subdued pace than, say, the barrelhouse boogie of 'Ready Teddy'.

Earl Palmer took the flak for this when he reflected on the track in 1999. The session drummer, who'd backed Fats Domino and underpinned Lloyd Price with military precision on 'Lawdy Miss Clawdy', explained that before he played on 'Tutti Frutti' at J&M, he'd been used to providing 'a shuffle or slow triplets' and credited Richard with introducing him to 'that straight eight-note feeling'. Palmer's instinct was to play the shuffling beat he'd brought to Domino's earlier records. 'But', he admitted, 'with Richard pounding the piano with all 10 fingers, you couldn't so very well go against that. I did at first. On "Tutti Frutti", you can hear me playing a shuffle. Listening to it now, it's easy to hear I should have been playing that rock beat.'

Palmer started out in his native New Orleans' fertile jazz scene but remade himself as a massively influential rock'n'roller in the wake of 'Tutti Frutti'. 'What I remember about those [Specialty] sessions is how physical they were', he said. 'You got to realise how Richard played. I'll tell you, the only reason I started playing what they come to call a rock'n'roll beat came from trying to match Richard's right hand. *Ding-ding-ding-ding*!'

Billy Vera notes that according to 'the Musician's Union contract in Specialty's files', the reassuringly named Huey 'Piano' Smith played piano on the single that blew David Bowie's mind. In 1989, though, Bumps Blackwell relayed what "really" went down after his and Richard's lunchtime jaunt to the Dew Drop Inn, following that unsuccessful initial session at J&M.

The producer explained that he and Richard ran through a couple of tracks while Dorothy LaBostrie rattled off the new, PG-rated lyrics for 'Tutti Frutti'. She presented them with '15 or 20 minutes' of the session remaining: 'I remember the musicians were packing up their horns and leaving. So I went up there and said, "Wait a minute. . ."' In *The Life and Times of Little Richard*, Blackwell claimed that the rush to record the tune with fifteen minutes on the studio clock meant 'it was impossible for other piano players to learn it in the short time we had', leaving the Southern Child to batter the keys himself.

If the race to change the world in two takes meant that Specialty didn't update the Musician's Union contract, the man who'd been booked to play piano that day wasn't exactly jealous. Smith, who would become celebrated for his own classics 'Don't You Just Know It' and 'Rockin' Pneumonia and the Boogie-Woogie Flu', didn't share Blackwell's enthusiasm for Richard's key-shattering style. 'Almost everybody plays music', he once groused. 'Hit on the piano and go, *"BUNGA! BUNGA! BUNGA!"* Say you do that on a record and it sells, what you gonna get somebody to play for? I guess since they started callin' that playin' the piano, that's when he became a pianist. But I played on the session before he became a piano player.'

Smith wasn't the only virtuoso to be shocked by Little Richard's brutal piano playing. 'I guess that thing that made "Long Tall Sally" was the way he broke up the piano', said J&M session man Edward Frank, who was paralyzed in one arm and could *still* claim to be a more elegant pianist than our hero. 'You know, they had to stop and get the tuner.'

Richard Penniman played piano the way punk bands would later play guitar: with little technical skill but a whole lot of feeling. His style had a profound effect on the young Elton John. 'You can't really say Jerry Lee [Lewis] didn't influence me either', says Elton, 'but Little Richard, for me . . . the way I play the piano is more similar to him than

Jerry Lee. Jerry Lee was an extraordinary piano player; Little Richard was just, like . . . the *power* that he played the piano with – wow!'

~

Decades since it was recorded, 'Tutti Frutti' still contains mysteries. Bumps Blackwell claimed he'd brought Dorothy LaBostrie along to the Dew Drop Inn when Richard ploughed through that super-sexy, early version of the song, before the producer hoiked them both back to J&M so that LaBostrie could scrub out all the references to shagging. In 1984, though, she told *Wavelength* magazine, whose writer described her as 'a spirited dark-skinned woman with Indian features', that she wrote the song from scratch herself.

'I was listening to the radio and an announcement came on that immediately caught my attention', she explained. 'It said that Bumps Blackwell was looking for songwriters. Well, as soon as I heard where he was gonna be, I decided I was gonna be a songwriter. I was working as a cook for a lady and I told her that I had to quit because I was going to write a record. She probably thought I was crazy, but that's exactly what I did.

'I practically broke Cosimo's door down the next day. Little Richard was sitting at the piano and it was the first time I'd ever laid eyes on him. I just asked to hear his voice and I sat down and put "Tutti Frutti" down on paper in 15 minutes.'

LaBostrie stuck by this story in 1995 when she was interviewed on TV and described Richard's lyrical style as 'nasty, nasty, nasty', adding: 'He would sing a dirty blues that would make your hair curl and I couldn't take it.' Here she claimed 'Tutti Frutti' actually began life as an ode to confectionery (rather than, y'know, anal lubrication): 'I already had the title of it because when my girlfriend and I went to the drugstore and I wanted vanilla ice cream, she said, "They got a new one." So I said, "Tutti frutti? Oh, rootie! Oh – I got a song." I throwed it on back in my mind.'

After she'd written the song, she recalled, '[Richard] stood at the piano. He never sat down to play – never. Not that I've ever seen! He went to banging, banging, hollering and then I took the song up and began to sing: *Wamp poma luma poma lump bam boom! Tutti frutti!*" See, I can sing the whole song completely through. So he couldn't take me a word from mine.'

LaBostrie was surprised, then, to find herself sharing the song's writing credit with Richard – though things looked better when Art Rupe called from LA to ask about her price for the work. The fledgling songwriter would have been happy with $50 to help her mother, who'd suffered a stroke, as she believed that 'was a whole lot of money'. Instead, she explained, 'He said, "No, you look for $500 in the morning" and he sent me $500. The next week, he sent another 500. When he sent me the big cheque, I got 2,450 dollars and 78 cents.'

Along with Blackwell, LaBostrie also co-wrote 'I'm Just a Lonely Guy', which became the B-side to 'Tutti Frutti'. Yet she contributed only one other song to Specialty Records, having co-authored the 1955 Li'l Millet and his Creoles flop 'Rich Woman'. She said this was because she refused to sign her royalties over to Rupe: 'He wanted to control everything.

They wanted more songs, but they wanted to pay me a flat $500 for them.'

Dorothy LaBostrie died in 2007, so never heard Robert Plant and Alison Krauss's cover of 'Rich Woman', which won them the Grammy for Best Pop Collaboration with Vocals in 2009. She'd continued to work as a songwriter until 1970 when she was hurt in a car accident and retreated from the music business.

In that *Wavelength* interview, she said she'd known not to forfeit her royalties because 'Tutti Frutti' had already served her so well by that point. For what was allegedly fifteen minutes' work, LaBostrie claimed she received a cheque for around $5,000 every three to six months. 'The last big one', she beamed, came to $30,000.

~

Cosimo Matassa once tactfully stated that both songwriters were correct to claim authorship of 'Tutti Frutti', remarking: 'Dorothy's a nice lady, but she gives herself more credit than she should.' In this regard, of course, Richard wasn't exactly scrupulous himself.

The *Here's Little Richard* album track 'Baby', for example, started life as a Billy Wright song called 'Don't You Want a Man Like Me?' It's nearly exactly the same tune, and yet Richard introduces a demo recording of his version as 'one that I've made'. On that demo, he asks, 'Baby, don't you wish your man had long hair like mine?', which is lifted almost word-for-word from Wright. This knowing campiness was excised from Richard's finished version, which is shamelessly credited solely to 'Penniman'. Like 'Tutti Frutti', the song was straightened out for the masses.

Richard's appropriation of 'Slippin' and Slidin'' is also extremely dubious, to say the least. At one point he said he'd been rehearsing the song 'in my room in Macon way before I started recording for Specialty'. At another, he explained that Wilbert 'Lee Diamond' Smith, a pianist and sax player in the Upsetters, 'gave me some of the words and I changed them around'. Actually, Ace Records' Al Collins released a languid early version of the tune, under the title 'I Got the Blues for You', in 1955. New Orleans bluesman Eddie Bo reworked it as the slightly pacier 'I'm Wise' the following year. Neither made much of a dent in history, but when Little Richard sprinkled his magic dust on the track, the result was a masterpiece that reached number two on the *Billboard* R&B chart. And at least he shares the songwriting credits on that one.

The Georgia Peach similarly claimed he wrote the melody to 'Ready Teddy', which is credited only to John Marascalco and Bumps Blackwell. Was the latter ever upset about these songwriting disputes? 'He just took it with a grain of salt and kept movin',' laughs Kelly Lee Blackwell. 'He knew Richard, and Richard had to be the star – all the time. And that was the good thing about daddy, because daddy knew to let him be the star. That's how it worked with them. So Bumps wasn't trippin' on nothin' like that.'

Perhaps having noticed that the '70s zeitgeist was blowing in the direction of the singer-songwriter, Richard told *Rolling Stone* in 1970: 'All my songs are experiences.' Here he alluded to 'Miss Ann', which he described elsewhere as an ode to Ann Howard, the aforementioned friend who took a young Richard in when Bud threw him out. Along with her husband Johnny, she co-owned Miss Ann's Tic-Toc club, a queer-friendly Macon joint where Richard and the Upsetters performed in their pre-fame days.

It was alleged among the venue's clientele that Ann and Richard were lovers, though he only went as far as claiming to have 'slept in the same bed between' she and her husband. With Little Richard, sometimes the rebuttal is weirder than the rumour. Based on his ragged vocals, though, the song certainly resembles a cry of passion: 'Woah-oh-woah, Miss Ann, you're doing something no-one can.' Billy Vera, meanwhile, points out that 'Miss Ann' was Black slang for an entitled white woman, suggesting the song is laced with a touch of subversive humour: 'I always felt that there was a little dig in there with that song – most likely.'

For all his tall tales, and regardless of whose name was on the credits, there's a reason Richard was the main attraction. Cosimo Matassa said of the Specialty sessions:

> [He] worked *fiendishly* hard. I mean *physically* hard. He really drove himself. Just like an artist gets from what the back-up guys play, it's the other way around, too. When you've got a Little Richard poundin' at the piano the way he did, singin' and drivin' the way he did, it had to make those guys play better. It had to make them give more of themselves, you know?

Richard and the band slogged through a comparatively breezy fourteen takes of 'Rip It Up'. The fourth finds an imperious singer in full flow as he casts that genius over the musicians, instructing them: 'Don't forget your solo now!

Aaaah! And just come in strong! And while you soloing, just keep that steady rhythm – just pound it. And just do all your little things. Just go mad, you know! Yes! Ready!'

~

One of the greatest contradictions around *Here's Little Richard* concerns 'Long Tall Sally', which is attributed to Richard, Blackwell and one Enotris Johnson; the latter is also named as a co-writer on 'Jenny, Jenny' and 'Miss Ann'.

Richard and the gang finally perfected 'Long Tall Sally' at J&M on 10 February 1956. This was just over two months after that abortive – and, for the singer, embarrassing – attempt in Los Angeles. On the finished product, he perfects the 'Hoo!' vocal tic he debuted on 'Tutti Frutti', which so inspired the Beatles and which he himself adapted from the '40s gospel great Mahalia Jackson. The track is sometimes listed with a curious titular appendage, 'The Thing', which was its original title. There was a film of the same name due for release, and Art Rupe had his eyes on its soundtrack. When that didn't pan out, he renamed the tune after lyrics that were, ultimately, just as weird.

Bumps Blackwell claimed Enotris Johnson was a teenage girl who had walked from 'Opelousas, Mississippi' to New Orleans with the sole purpose of showing him three lines of lyrics, which she'd scratched into a ratty piece of paper. 'Saw Uncle John with Long Tall Sally', they read. 'They saw Aunt Mary comin' / So they ducked back in the alley.' Enotris needed them to record the 'song', Blackwell said, because her real-life Aunt Mary was sick and required money for treatment. So he and Richard got to work, transforming the lines into a rock'n'roll classic.

Aside from the fact that this is a completely batshit story, we must also remember that Richard reckoned to have written 'Long Tall Sally' as a lowly dishwasher back at the Greyhound Bus Station kitchen in Macon; he said it was based on a larger-than-life woman from his childhood. The song's lyrics depict a 'baldhead Sally' who has 'everything that Uncle John need[s]' – and he's extremely keen that Aunt Mary doesn't find out about that. But wait a minute! Why is Sally bald? According to W. T. Lhamon, who expressed the idea in his book *Deliberate Speed: The Origins of a Cultural Style in the American 1950s*, it's because the character is a 'transvestite fantasy figure'. Well, Richard *did* spend his early years knocking about with mates who gleefully defied gender norms.

There's long been speculation, too, about the true identity of Enotris Johnson, given that Blackwell's tale seems so far-fetched. Some have suggested this was the name of Ann Howard's husband (in that *Rolling Stone* interview, Richard referred to her as 'Ann Johnson', which might have been where the rumour started). Another persistent theory has had it that Enotris Johnson was an adoptive father who came into Little Richard's life after Bud was killed, with Richard giving Johnson a co-writing credit in order to earn money for his mother. The truth, though, is an even better story.

The *real* Enotris Johnson was born in Hammond, Louisiana (not 'Opelousas, Mississippi', which doesn't even exist – though there is an Opelousas in Louisiana), on 3 October 1935. In 1956, having co-written those three timeless Little Richard tracks and a dozen other tunes, she disappeared from the music business. Her vanishing opened up a space for those crackpot theories to flourish for nearly six full decades. When she died on 2 August 2015, the truth finally came out. This brilliant Black songwriter, says Billy Vera, 'found religion, married a minister, and like so many show business people who get religion, they don't wanna talk about their days in [show business]'.

That minister was the Reverend Willie J. Johnson. According to a Facebook post shared by the Bogalusa Blues and Heritage Festival a week after her death, he was 'a good man' who asked 'that her work prior to their marriage remain private'. The festival's President Michelle Goode explains: 'Every year for the Bogalusa Blues & Heritage Festival we honour someone from our community that has an impact on the arts.' In 2015, that person was Enotris Johnson, who shared the billing with the Louisianan oil painter and art teacher Ann Warner.

As such, the festival displayed a board that bore Enotris's photograph and a short passage about her achievements. In the picture, taken in her later years, she looks regal in a buoyant lime green dress and headscarf, a pink flower pinned to her breast. 'In the early 1950s,' the caption reads, 'her zest for life and gift for songwriting combined', explaining that her family has now 'revealed her well-kept secret'. Along with Dorothy LaBostrie's work, it's a testament to the central role that Black women have played in the formation of rock'n'roll.

The tribute continues: 'Johnson supported her husband's ministry, and never claimed her fame publicly. She affectionately referred to her musical accomplishments as an "undercover operation", but near the end of her life began to speak of her song writing openly and with a great sense of humor. Johnson had no regrets. She experienced decades of marriage and ministry.

'And when she heard her lyrics sung by numerous artists over the years, she quietly thanked God for giving her the additional gift of song writing.'

'My God! Listen to that voice!'

9
Fame

Three decades after he heard God in 'Tutti Frutti', David Bowie was searching for the sound of tomorrow. It was an odyssey that resulted in 1983's *Let's Dance*, his best-selling album, which he co-produced with Nile Rodgers. 'David knocks on my door one day', recalls Rodgers, 'after we had been searching for what the vibe was gonna be on the record. He just showed me a picture of Little Richard: he had a reddish hue to his hair, getting into a red Cadillac. [Bowie] said: "Nile – I want my album to *sound* like this picture." And I knew *exactly* what he meant.'

'He didn't want a nostalgic record – no! Because when you saw that picture of Little Richard getting into this red Cadillac. . . . It was one of those older Cadillacs with the bullet tail lights and stuff, but it looked like it was from the future. And I realised David wanted a record that was evergreen: as old as that photograph was, it still looked modern and cool. He wanted a record that would be modern and cool in 100 years.'

Rodgers notes that the King and Queen 'could have taken that photo that morning, or he could have taken it today'. *Here's Little Richard*, too, sounds like the past, present and future of music all at once. It's a snapshot of the cultural eruptions that defined the United States in the 1950s and a glimpse at the artist leaps that can occur when a musician – such as, say, David Bowie – dares to live as limitlessly as Little Richard.

Rodgers doesn't know the current whereabouts of the photo, which would surely be an auctioneer's dream. 'Honestly', he sighs, 'I've tried to look for it. David had incredible resources, so I'm not really sure where he got it.' The disco don, though, believes the picture depicts the Georgia Peach on the road: 'In those days, sometimes people would take photos just to do a concert. Like, a person would come to town and they'd do a photo session; they'd make a poster and all sorts of stuff.'

Given this supposition, along with the fact it features a bullet tail-light-adorned Cadillac, an icon of the '50s, it seems likely the picture was taken between 1955 and 1957, when the star was in his pomp. No one has ever been more alive than Little Richard was in this era. If the image radiates transgressive energy, it's perhaps not unrelated to the way in which he and the Upsetters were challenging the status quo on a nightly basis.

On tour in the South at the height of their fame, the band faced all the same problems they'd encountered on the Chitlin' Circuit in the early '50s. Saxophonist Grady Gaines recalled:

'When we got on the East Coast and in certain parts of California, we felt like we were in God's country.' In 1957, as part of one booking in Louisiana, the Upsetters played a daytime show for a Black audience in the gym of McKinley High School in Baton Rouge and a night-time gig for the white crowd at Cal's Club in Prairieville. Although this was common practice at the time, Richard would proudly boast about his fans' defiance of Jim Crow. 'At some of the shows I did in the early days', he said, 'when I was drawing more blacks . . . the white people would jump over the balcony and come.'

His sometime arranger and sax player H. B. Barnum marvelled at these rock'n'roll rebellions: 'Richard opened the door. He brought the races together. When I first went on the road there were many segregated audiences. With Richard, although they still had the audiences segregated in the building, they were *there* together. And most times, before the end of the night, they would all be mixed together.'

It was Richard who paid the price for this. On one such occasion (which might have been the same incident in Texas that Charles Connor remembered), he was summoned to court to answer for the so-called disturbance. 'The judge asked me what did I have to say for myself', he said. '"What do I have to say for myself? Everything!" And he said: "Order in the court!" I said: "That's what you need in here. I haven't seen any of that since I've been here!" And so he told me if I did that one more time, they were going to put me out – they were going to lock me up. He told me I was crazy. I'll never forget that.'

Because he was Little Richard, and his natural instinct was to bring joy, he turned the tale into a cartoon: 'He told me my hair was too long. He says: "Are you a man? What *are* you?"'

~

Through all of this prejudice, Richard and the band never seemed to be having any less than an absolute blast. Where Elvis and his backing group, the Blue Moon Boys, began to drift as the King found success, with guitarist Scotty Moore disgruntled at being sidelined, the Upsetters and their singer remained as solid as a waxed-up pompadour.

'The band was so close and warm', said Charles Connor. 'We used to walk down the street with our arms around Richard, and that made people love us, to see that the band was good, warm friends. We used to get respect out of black and white, like we were heroes.'

Richard longed to record in the studio with his beloved Upsetters: here was another long-standing wedge between him and a resistant Art Rupe. '[The Upsetters] was the rockingest group on the road at the time', the frontman later enthused. 'They dressed fabulously, and were one of the few groups that was choreographed. They were good-looking guys and fantastic musicians. In fact, I haven't heard nothing like them to this day.'

If the Beatles invented the concept of the rock band as an autonomous entity and did so with their final line-up in 1962, the Upsetters put on a united front nearly a decade earlier. Connor revealed that Richard and the lads would head to a 'beauty shop' to get their hair done together, a deeply enjoyable detail that's also pretty sobering, given how dangerous it was for a Black man to be in any way flamboyant in the mid-'50s. There must have been a thin line between evading trouble – as they leaned into their unthreatening, outlandish image – and inviting it.

When Connor remembered that the Upsetters dressed campily so as not to seem a temptation to white women who might 'shower' them with 'panties', he added, with an indulgent chuckle, 'We were no threat – or they *thought* we were no threat.' Richard claimed that women would write their phone numbers on naked photos of themselves and throw them onstage, and that he and the band revelled in raucous orgies together after shows, booking out entire top floors of hotels to accommodate the party.

He enjoyed his own brand of Beatlemania in the *Here's Little Richard* era – predominantly in the United States, though the blast waves reached Canada and ricocheted back to Australia via the Philippines, all of which he toured. Asked, in that blockbuster 1970 *Rolling Stone* interview, how many 'rock'n'roll riots' he'd witnessed in this period, Richard replied: 'Oh my God – every one I played, I saw one. They had to ease me out in trucks. I came out as janitors; I've been everything.'

After the McKinley High School show in Baton Rouge, overwhelmed fans upturned Richard's Cadillac as he attempted to pull away from the venue. 'It was wild', promoter Charlie Carter said in 1998. 'They called out the police to control the students.' There was no support act for Richard and the Upsetters on the American tour: 'We didn't need anybody with Little Richard in those days', Carter explained.

'Every place was a sell-out.' The promoter dubbed the show 'explosive, top-of-the-line entertainment', raving: 'Like with Elvis, [the audiences] were at the stage. They screamed and hollered, and they would follow the car when he got ready to pull off.'

Grady Gaines described the pandemonium Richard incited as 'the greatest rock'n'roll show ever', adding: 'It was like just you ran into a tornado or something.'

The press agreed. 'Wildly enthusiastic scenes greeted each and every performance by the . . . five-foot-nothing "rock" star in Canada', roared *NME* on 20 September 1957. The audience rushed the stage in Victoria, British Columbia; Richard hunkered down in his motel room in Nanaimo, Vancouver Island, as rock'n'roll fans surrounded the building. 'At Vancouver', the report continued, 'several girls collapsed as a result of the tremendous crush around the bandstand.'

~

That wide-eyed article had Little Richard announcing that 'rock'n'roll is a "rage which is part of teenage life"'. But whose teenage life? John Waters once described the genre as a Black movement with 'the cool white kids loving it and the less cool white kids listening to the cover when the white groups would do it'.

These white artists' steadier covers habitually outsold the source material, even though they stripped away the transgressive energy that made the songs so exciting in the first place. Nashville crooner Pat Boone, who is often cast as a villain of this tale, covered 'Tutti Frutti' when Richard's was still in the charts. His anaemic swing version is almost comically naff, so far removed from the tune's sexed-up origins that he turns Daisy into a 'real gone cookie'. But that didn't stop Boone from taking the song to number twelve on *Billboard*'s pop chart, with the Originator's stuck at twenty-one.

'A lot of white acts were capitalising on a lot of black songs', says Tom Jones, 'with Elvis Presley being the prime example with his early stuff. He was just doing what black people were doing. Pat Boone covered "Ain't That A Shame" by Fats Domino, and then Bill Haley did "Rip It Up", "Shake, Rattle and Roll" – a bunch of [songs] that had been done by black artists.' Often the more commercially successful white versions were more available than the originals: 'We didn't hear them, you see.'

Jones remembers precisely when he first heard Little Richard. He was at the Park Hall cinema in Pontypridd with his wife Linda Trenchard, who sadly passed away in 2016. 'We were courting at the time', he says. 'It was just before we got married in the '50s.' The Park Hall was one of three Pontypridd cinemas that Linda's family owned: 'It was great because we could go to the pictures for nothing!' As the projectionist changed the reels between film, a voice screamed over the speakers: 'IT'S SATURDAY NIGHT AND I JUST GOT PAID! FOOL ABOUT MY MONEY! DON'T TRY TO SAVE!'

'The only version of "Rip It Up" that I'd heard to that point was by Bill Haley and the Comets', explains Jones. 'I didn't know anybody else had recorded it. . . . *This* voice came on, singing 'Rip It Up'. *Right!* I said to my wife, 'Who the *hell* is that!? I mean, it's not Bill Haley and the Comets.' I thought maybe it was a girl because Little Richard had a very high voice (he was a tenor, so he was up there). You couldn't tell because nobody [announced the artist] – they just played the record. I said, 'My God! Listen to that *voice*! That's unbelievable!'

Jones marched to his local record shop and demanded, 'Who else has done "Rip It Up"?' The answer was a revelation: 'Right from there I started buying his records.' He was able to do so thanks to London Records, who distributed US releases in the UK – and vice versa – for Decca Records; the label issued 'Rip It Up' for the British market in November 1956, six months after its release in the States. '[Richard's version of "Rip It Up"]', Jones notes, 'was tremendous because it was so different. It was more different than the Bill Haley one, which was a very good record. But Little Richard, when you hear him do it...'

Pat Boone also covered 'Rip It Up' in 1956, as well as 'Long Tall Sally'. Richard expressed mixed feelings about this appropriation of his tunes. 'When Pat Boone came out', he admitted in 1987, 'man, I was mad. I was going to go to Nashville and find him. I wasn't kidding at the time, because he was stomping my progress. I wanted to be famous and here this man done came and took my song.'

It was true, however, that Boone's version introduced 'Tutti Frutti' to white listeners, helping the song to achieve its crossover success in the pop chart. Although Richard was initially furious at Boone's pale imitation, he came to feel that he and other white musicians helped to desegregate the charts. 'It took people like Elvis and Pat Boone, Gene Vincent', he said in 1970, 'to open the door for this kind of music.'

Still, Blackwell claimed he and Richard deliberately set 'Long Tall Sally' at a breakneck pace to outfox Boone: 'After making ["Tutti Frutti"] and then being covered by Pat Boone and being smothered by promotion and all, it didn't make me very happy. So I said, "OK – I'll get you on this next one."' Richard added: 'I rehearsed that line, you know, *"ducked-back-in-the-alley"*, with Bumps for hours until we got it like a drumbeat. You know – *"da-da-da-da-da-da."*'

The tactic worked, as the original reached number six on the *Billboard* pop chart, the cover number eight. Little wonder: Boone's version of 'Long Tall Sally' is even more ridiculous than his 'Tutti Frutti'. Richard was right when he boasted that his rival 'couldn't get his mouth around the words'. Where the original erupts and flows with volcanic passion, Boone's attempt at 'Long Tall Sally' is soft, inoffensive and bland – the very definition of 'white bread'.

'That's the first version I heard', chuckles Tom Jones, 'the Pat Boone [cover]. And then you hear Little Richard and you think, "Jesus Christ! What the fuck is that!"'

~

The Welsh superstar wasn't the only British music fan hungry for a bite of the Georgia Peach. In November 1956, shortly before London Records released 'Rip It Up' in the UK, a frustrated 'G. Greenwood of Guycroft, Otley, Yorks' wrote into the *NME* letters page and demanded: 'When are we going to be able to obtain Little Richard's records in Britain? After hearing his versions of "Long Tall Sally", "Slippin' An' [*sic*] Slidin'" and "Ready Teddy", I think he is one of the best artists the rock 'n' roll trend has produced.'

These ripples across the pond were nothing compared to the impact Little Richard was having on his homeland. His influence on pop music is, as we've seen, impossible to overestimate – but it's still surprising to see where you end up after following the thread of his genius. For example: Little Richard invented the disco beat. And he did it in the mid-'50s, some twenty years before Donna Summer moaned and groaned her way through 'Love to Love You Baby'.

That's according to Charles Connor, anyway, who recalled that the frontman requested extra oomph when the Upsetters rocked the tune out on the road. Like Earl Palmer himself, Richard was dissatisfied with the percussion on the recorded track. Connor explained: 'Richard said to us, "I want 'Tutti Frutti' to have a lot more energy to it. I don't want just that single back-beat like when Earl Palmer played it in the studio." He made me change so it was more heavy on the bass drum.' Connor hadn't heard a sound like it – and wouldn't for another two decades. 'When I think of it now', he realized in 1984, 'it sounded almost like what's known as the disco beat.'

What does our resident disco Queen reckon to this? Might Little Richard have had a perfumed hand in the formation of the genre? 'I can say that', replies Candi Staton, 'because he was very creative. But, you know, [artists] do a lot of things that we don't get credit for. I don't doubt that at all, that they took that beat.'

Just as he worked '*fiendishly* hard' at J&M Recording Studio, the Architect had the Upsetters rehearse relentlessly. Connor claimed they derived their name from the fact 'we were supposed to upset every town we played in', revealing that Richard insisted: "'If another band jumps off the stage, I want you to jump off the roof of the house!'"

He's often portrayed as an impulsive wildman who *did* instead of thought, but Little Richard had a lot more agency than that. There was further evidence of this vision in the 1960s, when he could be credited with discovering a pre-fame Jimi Hendrix and The Beatles' future secret weapon Billy Preston, both of whom joined his live band – indeed, Preston first met the Fab Four at their Hamburg shows with the Quasar in '62.

Thanks to his talent, hard work and unique way of looking at the world, Richard Penniman lifted himself from a one-storey house in Pleasant Hill, Macon, Georgia, attaining a level of superstardom that shaped the very world we live in. Like a modern celebrity, he was so famous he even had his own brand of perfume: Princess Cherri. By 1957, he'd moved his family to Hollywood, incited Pennimania on at least three continents and evaded crazed fans in a Cadillac just like the one Lloyd Price pulled up to the Macon City Auditorium in all those years ago. Hell, he'd even recruited the drummer who played on 'Lawdy Miss Clawdy' and helped him to invent a whole new style.

And as the year neared its close, the 24-year-old found himself being prepared to ship out to Sydney, Australia, some 9,000 miles from his hometown. Here he would play a cavernous stadium to 40,000 hysterical fans for whom such a spectacle could have been nothing but brain-devouring, given that it barely existed at the time. You couldn't blame the man for having such bad vertigo that he wanted to hit the ejector seat.

'God doesn't like it'

10
Can't Believe You Wanna Leave

The Sydney Stadium crowd was growing restless, but Little Richard had more important things to worry about. He'd arrived onstage fresh from four sold-out Australia shows as part of a package tour that also featured Eddie Cochran and Alis Lesley, who was dubbed 'the female Elvis Presley' (the King himself reportedly recommended her for the gig). A photo of the three tour mates, taken shortly after they arrived at Sydney airport on 28 September, graces the cover of Bob Dylan's 2022 book *The Philosophy of Modern Song*. They look bright with promise: Cochran cocksure, Lesley deadpan and Richard grinning cheekily.

By 12 October, as he defiantly faced down 40,000 bewildered fans who stomped their feet in anticipation of 'Long Tall Sally', the look on Richard's face had turned to righteous ire. 'If you want to live with the Lord,' he exclaimed, 'you can't rock'n'roll too! God doesn't like it.'

He had hinted for some time about his scheme to split the Devil's nightclub and dedicate himself to God's word.

'We were not really too surprised', said Charles Connor, who explained that the frontman alluded to the vow 'whenever he got down in the dumps'.

Four months before the Sydney show, *Melody Maker* reported on rumours that 'the chanter may give up the rock'n'roll field entirely for evangelism'. The whispers continued that September when *NME* warned: 'The music world may be losing Little Richard very soon. During his recent successful tour of Canada, he appeared at Vancouver's Exhibition Gardens on June 12 and surprised reporters by announcing his intention of deserting the bright lights of show business in the near future to become an evangelist.'

And then it finally happened. The Sydney audience came expecting the wildest rock'n'roller of them all, the man of indeterminate sexuality, slathered in make-up, pounding his way through some of the filthiest songs ever recorded, and instead found themselves subjected to a sermon. Richard finished the gig half-heartedly; he was done with being Upsetter-in-Chief.

The headline in *NME*'s 8 November issue duly screamed: 'SHOCK FOR ROCK 'N' ROLL WORLD – *LITTLE RICHARD PACKS IT UP!*' An accompanying article breathlessly rammed home the point that 'Little Richard has quit! He's given up show business and will devote his life to evangelism. In future he will only make spiritual records.' Just in case there was still ambiguity in the matter, the writer assured the reader: 'He is finished with pop and rock disks.'

~

True to the unreliable narrator we know, Richard's version of what happened in Australia shifted over the years. There's his well-documented claim that he saw a fireball soar over Sydney Stadium that night and knew it to be a warning from God. And its well-documented rebuttal: that what he'd actually seen was Sputnik, the first-ever artificial Earth satellite, which the Soviet Union had launched just eight days before Richard's vision.

The vessel sent radio signals back to the planet for twenty-two days, continued in orbit for another two months and violently re-entered the Earth's atmosphere on 4 January 1958, by which time Brother Richard was a fully signed-up member of the Seventh-day Adventist Church who'd enrolled at Oakwood University, Alabama. He joined the Black Christian university to study in earnest for the Ministry (though admittedly arrived on campus in a less than ascetic yellow Cadillac).

Richard relayed his alternative – and similarly outlandish – account of these events to *Melody Maker* in 1962. His epiphany occurred, he said, when the Holy Spirit commandeered a malfunctioning plane for him and flew it to safety: 'I was flying to a concert in the Philippines and the engine of the plane caught fire. I prayed for it and God did it. That was how my life changed.' Curiously, Charles Connor has endorsed at least *some* of this yarn. 'The captain got on the PA system', the drummer recalled, '[and said], "Don't worry – everything will be OK because we can fly with three engines."'

Whether that plane was landed by the Lord God or an aviation expert is a question for the Air Line Pilots

Association, but the result was that Richard walked away from a legally binding label contract with another lucrative tour lined up. Instead of fulfilling his commitments, the rock star reportedly made a grand gesture in Australia to prove he meant it, man: 'We got on a ferry', Richard claimed decades later, 'and I said, "Well, if you don't believe I'm going to stop, I'll throw all my diamonds in the ocean." And I threw all my big rings in the water.'

It sounds like more Richard bunkum but the story has, again, been co-signed by a contemporary, even if the action moved from a ferry to a bridge. In 1962, Gene Vincent, who shared the bill on that Australian date, too, explained to *NME*: 'When somebody challenged the seriousness of what he was going to do, [he] stood on the bridge of Sydney Harbour – I was there beside him – and took £8,000 worth of rings off his finger and threw them into the river (I nearly jumped in after them, I can tell you!).'

~

There are, naturally, also multiple theories as to why Little Richard *really* committed what looks a lot like a serious act of career self-harm, abandoning rock'n'roll at the height of his fame, sacrificing millions of dollars and immeasurable personal validation, as well as inviting all manner of legal drama.

Whichever way you cut it, though, our story ends almost as soon as it began. By mid-1958, rock'n'roll had imploded: Elvis was absent in the Army; Jerry Lee Lewis was cancelled for marrying his 13-year-old cousin, Myra Gale Brown; and Little Richard had found God.

Yes, it's possible that the latter was simply so overwhelmed by his new life in the pompadour-singing spotlight, and by the controversy caused by rock'n'roll, that he craved the comfort and moral certainty of the church. After all, imagine how a dirt-poor kid from Macon, Georgia, must have felt in the blinding glare of twentieth-century celebrity when he barely even understood what it was. Perhaps, too, flush with fame, he felt the world would wait for him. But by the time Richard released his rock'n'roll comeback album *Little Richard Is Back! (And There's a Whole Lotta Shakin' Goin' On!)* in 1964, the Beatles had changed everything.

Additionally, it's been reported that Richard was under scrutiny from the Inland Revenue Service and that this made the Ministry – along with its tax-free status – look very inviting indeed. R&B-star-turned Christian evangelist Joe Lutcher, a Specialty artist, may have also borne some responsibility. Billy Vera explains that Lutcher 'convinced [Richard] that he should get religion [by saying], "You're a sinner," 'cause he was living a pretty wild life'. John Marascalco, on the other hand, reckoned the revelation was a bid to escape that half-cent royalty rate: 'Richard told me when he came back from Australia that he was going to break that contract with Specialty. He said, "The only way I can do it is if I die or by an act of God."'

Whatever the true reason for the contrarian rock star's most confounding move, he bundled the band back on a flight to the United States a week-and-a-half before the tour was originally intended to end. In what was perhaps an attempt to justify a career kamikaze mission that shocked so many around him, he claimed the plane they were scheduled to fly home on duly collided with the ocean. Richard Kebabjian, who collates aviation disasters for the website planecrashinfo .com, 'could not find any accident involving a commercial airliner going from Australia to the US in 1957'.

For all the furore he'd caused, Richard was nothing if not single-minded on the matter. In a moment of uncertainty, ahead of the Sydney show, he invited the Seventh-day Adventist Church Pastor J. B. Conley to meet him in his Melbourne hotel room. Here he outlined the quandary posed by the quarter-of-a-million-dollars-a-year deal that stood between him and God. And it was here that Conley finally convinced him that the only option was to break the contract.

'Well', Richard mused, 'There will be Hell to pay.' 'Let Hell come', Conley replied. 'Christ conquered Hell.'

~

Back on Planet Earth, the lag between the King and Queen's onstage abdication and that hysterical *NME* headline was down, in part, to Art Rupe having entered what we might now call 'crisis PR mode'.

The vexed mogul persuaded Richard not to announce his news when he returned to America. He also managed to squeeze one more studio session from his unruly protégé, though it seemed the rock'n'roll blaze had been momentarily doused with Holy Water. The seven sides that the Upsetters laid down at Los Angeles' Master Recorders on October 18, which included the deliriously camp, Penniman-penned

'Ooh! My Soul!', were some distance from the well-drilled perfection of *Here's Little Richard*. After one emotional farewell show at New York's Apollo Theatre, the Living Flame was – for now – snuffed out.

Yet Rupe resolved to keep the Richard product coming. Specialty put out three massive Little Richard singles in the first half of 1958: an earlier, tighter take of 'Ooh! My Soul!', the cutesy 'Baby Face' and the electrifying 'Good Golly, Miss Molly'. Things became so desperate Rupe even released the original version of 'I Got It' as a (flop) single in 1959.

While the businessman struggled to keep the gravy train running, though, Richard was trying to prise it off the track. He wandered the grounds of Oakwood University, offering to purchase Little Richard records from any student who might possess them – and for more than they'd originally paid in-store. 'He wanted to have a bonfire by the bell tower in the middle of the campus and burn them all', said DeWitt S. Williams, who was a freshman at the time and remembered his peers cashing in on the offer: 'They went to the record stores, bought some of his records and let Little Richard buy them back at his special rate.'

If the prodigal son had swapped one form of exploitation for another, Rupe was determined to keep it quiet. Specialty did issue the papers with a brief statement to tie in with the Apollo show, explaining that Richard would 'work for Jehovah and find that peace of mind', but this did little to quell the stream of questions that flooded the label boss. Rumours swirled that his biggest star had killed himself or been committed to a mental health facility; Rupe and his employees blocked all inquiries on the matter.

In March 1959, the mogul turned the situation to his advantage with *The Fabulous Little Richard*, which was comprised of leftovers from the unrepeatable 1955 to 1957 era. The record's blurb made the fanciful claim that the singer had personally 'added voices on several of these numbers, bringing him closer to the type of church singing he was brought up on, and to which he is now returning'. In reality, it was not unlike a modern label releasing a posthumous album made up of a rapper's sketchy Voice Memos.

Rupe also effectively appointed Larry Williams as Little Richard's understudy while he waited for all this to blow over. The New Orleans singer and pianist recreated the Georgia Peach's sound and style to such an extent that his 1958 tune 'Short Fat Fannie' opens with lyrics about 'slippin' and a-slidin' with Long Tall Sally'.

In further proof that you never know where our hero's story is going, Larry Williams became Little Richard's drug dealer in the late '70s. They were both very much on the skids and when the King and Queen of Rock'n'roll fell behind on his payments, Williams threatened him with a pistol. The incident was partly what scared Richard into getting clean; Williams died in 1980 from a gunshot wound to the head, and there's debate over whether it was suicide or murder.

~

Four years after Williams's death, Little Richard took Art Rupe to court for a second time, citing $112 million in unpaid royalties. Although he had reportedly earned only

$25,000 from 'Tutti Frutti' even after the song exceeded half a million sales back in 1957, the Georgia Peach settled out of court for an undisclosed sum.

He had first sued in early 1959, by which time the label boss had withheld $11,000 worth of royalties in the wake of Sydney revelation. When Richard returned to the studio, Rupe said, he would cough up. The mogul remained bullish throughout the dispute but backed down when the case reached the California Superior Court, agreeing to pay on the proviso that Richard give up his publishing and songwriting entitlements. Lamentably, the singer agreed.

Rupe was not simply the villain here, insists Billy Vera:

> Richard got this religious conversion eighteen months into a three-year contract . . . Art explained to him: 'Richard, this puts you into breach of contract. I can't make you sing – and I certainly can't make you sing well – but if you keep doing what you're doing you'll be a millionaire many times over.' [Richard] said, 'I don't care, I don't wanna sing the Devil's music. I wanna just sing for God now.' So reluctantly [Rupe] said, 'Well, there is a price to be paid for breaking the contract.'

The mogul, of course, didn't *have* to enforce those sanctions – he chose to. Despite all of this, the rock star and the man who had discovered him retained a certain level of warmth throughout their lives – even if Richard would habitually bash Rupe in interviews. 'They spoke over the years', says Vera, though adds that they didn't do so very often. 'When [Richard] spoke with Art, he was more than civil – they were friendly – but when it was in public, [he] became the Richard that we know.'

In the early '60s, after Rupe had shut down Specialty, Richard implored him to sign the hot new act he'd met while blazing the rock'n'roll comeback trail in Germany, explains Vera: 'He said, "They can sound like anybody – even me!" And that was The Beatles. Art wasn't interested. He said: "I'm not in the business any more but if you wanna make a record yourself, I'll be happy to record you." Richard took Rupe up on his counter-offer, and the result was the tatty "Bama Lama Bama Loo".'

That song might have been self-parody at best but was ultimately borne of Richard Penniman's steadfast desire to help people – even the Beatles. When he renounced show business in October 1957, prior to Art Rupe banning him from talking to the press, Richard told an Australian radio station: 'I wanna study [religion] so I can help the other people that are doing wrong, where they can be saved too . . . I got to get completely from [rock'n'roll] to dedicate my life directly to God.'

What sinners' life was he referring to? That of being hauled before a judge and asked to answer for shaking his hips 'like a crazy man'? Of his shame at all the mixed-sex orgies, of the peepin' and a-hidin' that made him an outcast from the city that raised him? Could Little Richard never slip from his father's shadow, no matter how much love and joy and exhilaration he may generate?

Perhaps, some nights, when he roared 'A-wop-bop-a-loo-bop-a-lop-bam-boom', he was screaming into the void.

'So basic, so original, so early'

Epilogue

And yet.

Little Richard's tumultuous twenty-four months at the centre of the universe may have been largely defined – driven, even – by the tension between religion and rock'n'roll, but his legacy is all about rabble-rousing, rippin' it up and flyin' high, walkin' out unto the sky. He took the pain in his heart, the self-doubt that loomed over him, and turned them into songs that make you want to dance until your legs give out. Some rock music is a positive conduit for rage; his debut album is a toast to the sillier side of life, a hymn to happiness.

So it's little wonder he would turn his talents back to gospel, to a celebration of someone even bigger than life. Little Richard, though, was everything. This morality-obsessed, God-fearing man was also, according to John Waters, 'the first punk' – well, he did play piano like one. And because he was everything, he was also the opposite of a punk. 'I was the first [hippie]', he announced in 1970. 'I was the first one, 'cause I've been wearing the long hair and fancy clothes. I've been doing it all my life!' Here, too, was the artist who invented the disco beat and the first glam rocker, a gender-bending supernova.

'I didn't take from Richard consciously', says Joan Jett, 'but his music was so basic, so original, so early in the process of defining rock'n'roll, that Little Richard influenced all rock music that came afterwards – including me.'

If you need further evidence that Little Richard was the first punk rocker, just look at the fact that the Sex Pistols' Sid Vicious – the punkest and most controversial of the punks – spent much of 1977 wearing a T-shirt emblazoned with his image. But as we've seen, the space between rebellion and faith is narrower than you might think. Dave Grohl, asked to name his favourite Little Richard song, hovers around 'Keep-A-Knockin'' ('That's the jam! Not to mention that Led Zeppelin totally lifted the drum intro for that song for "Rock and Roll" . . .') before eventually arriving at 'Precious Lord'.

You might remember this song from Chapter 2 – it's the gospel number Richard sang in old folks' homes as a child, when his Uncle Willard drove him around Georgia to bring joy as part of the pint-sized group Tiny Tots. It was originally published in 1938 and written by the Christian evangelist Thomas A. Dorsey, who adapted the arrangement from a nineteenth-century hymn. Dorsey was inspired to write his new, redemptive version when his friend, the guitarist Tampa Red, succumbed to alcoholism after his wife and child died in a car accident. 'When my light is almost gone', the lyrics' wayward narrator implores a higher power, 'Hear my cry, hear my call / Hold my hand, lest I fall.'

Richard recorded the song for his first religious album *Pray Along with Little Richard*, which was released in 1960 when he was in immediate recovery from his life as a rock'n'roll sinner. 'The lyrics are beautiful', says Grohl. 'It's a gospel standard, but to hear him sing it is really beautiful.' As Little Richard 'was also Lemmy's hero', Grohl recited the song's lyrics at the Mötorhead frontman's funeral in 2016. '[It's] the one that always gets me.'

Around the 'late '90s, early 2000s', the Foo Fighter met Richard himself:

> I had always said, 'If there would be one person I would wanna meet, it would be Little Richard because without Little Richard, there'd be no rock'n'roll.' I met him outside of [Los Angeles International Airport]. I was standing outside smoking a cigarette and a young man came up to me and said, 'Are you Dave Grohl?' I said, 'Yes'. He said, 'I read that the only person you ever wanted to meet was Little Richard.' I said, 'Yeah – he's the Originator.'

The young man turned out to be Danny Jones Penniman, who'd become Richard's adopted son in 1984. He told Grohl that the Originator was 'sitting in the car right over there' and suggested: 'Let's go and say hello.'

'I put out my cigarette', says Grohl, 'we walked over, he taps on the window. The window came down and fucking Little Richard was sitting right there. And he looked at me and said' – cue an impressively high-pitched Little Richard impression to rival Tom Jones's – "God bless you, David. How are you?" He knew who I was! We were introduced and then he signed this postcard-sized, Bible pamphlet. It said:

"David
God cares
Little Richard"

He handed it to me and it was my most prized possession. . . .
At Lemmy's funeral, I told that story and then I pulled that
card out of my pocket and I put it on Lemmy's altar.'

Grohl describes the encounter as 'one of the most amazing
experiences of my life'. In his later years, Little Richard
seemed to relish wowing the rock stars he'd inspired to pick
up the guitar or pound at the piano.

Elton John, for example, pretty much starts and ends his
fabulous 2019 autobiography *Me* by reflecting on Richard's
role in his life. The conclusion to a revised, post-pandemic
version of the book sees him recall the day Little Richard died.
Elton spent the evening playing his records and remembering
the first time he ever saw the Georgia Peach perform live.
Referring to his given name, he wrote: 'Reg Dwight might
have been born in Pinner in 1947, but Elton John was born in
the stalls of the Harrow Granada that night in October 1962.'

The Rocket Man was amazed, then, to actually perform
with his hero at the Beverley Hilton hotel in Los Angeles. 'I
couldn't believe I was playing with him', Elton admits. 'When
you get to play with those kinds of people that you love so
much – and especially someone from the '50s that started it
all. . .' He trails off, shaking his head in disbelief.

Even now, all these years after that night at the Harrow
Granada, Elton speaks about Little Richard like a deity. 'Every
time you saw him', he says, 'you just fell in love with him. And

that smile, and the way he looked. He was so handsome and debonair. The way he dressed, and his cheeky smile – he was just . . . he was the Mohammad Ali of the piano.'

In fact, Billy Vera pinpoints the way in which Richard arguably became a victim of his own success as a pianist. 'This may sound like a stupid excuse', he told this writer for *NME* in 2021, 'but after The Beatles and the Stones and all those became popular, you had to almost be a guitar player to be taken seriously. . . . People came to associate rock'n'roll with guitar.'

It was the Architect's innovation in the *Here's Little Richard* era that paved the way for the British Invasion of the early '60s, which he hitched a wagon to when he made his comeback to rock'n'roll. In 1964, he appeared on the TV show *American Bandstand* and, clutching a photo of himself with the Fab Four, sagely informed host Dick Clark that he 'toured with The Beatles right before they made their first hit'. He added, bashfully, 'I was the star of the show . . . you wouldn't believe it.'

If the King and Queen seemed somewhat reduced in that appearance, declaring himself 'grateful' to see British bands covering his '50s hits, he'd rediscovered his ego by the '70s and '80s, when he'd appear on similar talk shows and make no bones about outlining exactly what was owed to him. He was invited back into the mainstream to co-present a gong at the Grammy Awards in 1988. Instead of being grateful, he hijacked the event. 'The Best New Artist', he said with a devilish glance, only pretending to look at the envelope that contained the answer, 'is . . . *me!* I have never received nothin'! You all ain't never gave me no Grammy! I am the Architect of Rock'n'roll! You ain't never gave me nothin'!'

The parallels to Kanye West interrupting Taylor Swift's acceptance speech at the 2009 MTV Video Music Awards are obvious. Unlike Kanye, though, Richard brought down the house and received a standing ovation. In this period, says Nile Rodgers, 'he was just so much fun to be around because he had great stories and great wit . . . he was fearless. He would just say what was on his mind.'

Still, it might sound a little tragic, the greatest rock star ever compelled to remind the world of all he'd afforded it. But can you blame the Architect for stating the obvious? He became the custodian of his own massive contribution to Planet Earth, his main role to remind everyone that Little Richard is always around us.

'When I became friendly with [him]', Rodgers says, 'he was much more a "personality" at that point. That's what I believe is the ultimate artist dream or goal. I don't know if they think like that, but to me that's the pinnacle of artistry where, after you've done your biggest and best work, it's just important for you to walk into the room.' In bigging himself up, the disco don adds, Richard was 'giving you his vocal account of real history'.

After all, as Kelly Lee Blackwell says of Richard and her father's mid-'50s legacy: 'What they did together was something truly, truly big. I don't think that's ever going to be captured again.'

It would be wrong, however, to say the innovator simply stalled in 1957. 'I didn't just love [him] on Specialty', says Elton John. 'I moved on with him: "I Don't Know What

You've Got (But It's Got Me)", which was a kind of gospel record, was one of my favourite records from that time.' Elton has proudly played this 'kind of bizarre, unheard-of Little Richard track', from 1965, on his Apple Music radio show *Rocket Hour*. Tom Jones, meanwhile, recommends the religious 1961 album *The King of the Gospel Singers*, which was produced by Quincy Jones: 'You should listen to it because it's tremendous.'

After his 1962 comeback, Richard spent decades batting between the sacred and the secular, unable to reconcile the two. He'd repeatedly quit rock'n'roll, then return when he needed the money. The guilt may well have contributed to the $1,000-a-day PCP, heroin and cocaine addiction he suffered and somehow overcame in the late-'70s. Eventually, though, he found a way to combine his enduring passions and fondly called 1986's *Lifetime Friend*, a loveable and accessible Christian rock record, 'message music'. Released shortly after the death of his deeply religious mother, who had implored him to stay with the Lord, this would be his final proper album of original material. He had solved the riddle of his life.

Little Richard duly received a belated Lifetime Achievement Award at the Grammys in 1993. It was the least they could do. 'I think he deserved every accolade he got', says Candi Staton. 'And some!' He was touring as late as 2013, when declining health caused him to give up the stage for good. In 2019, as Little Richard's enormous life began to wind down and a botched hip operation left him largely confined to his room at the Hilton Nashville Downtown hotel, where he chose to live, Tom Jones paid his old friend a visit.

'I flew to Nashville and saw [him]', says Jones. 'His son was downstairs in the hotel, so I talked to Richard on the phone. First of all, he tried to make out that it wasn't him! You know, he was going' – here comes that impression again – '"*Well, Mr. Penniman isn't seeing anybody at the moment.*" I said, "Richard – I know it's you!"'

Richard protested, 'I don't have my wig and I don't have any makeup', to which Jones replied: 'I don't give a fuck about your . . . I wanna see *you!*' When the Living Flame eventually agreed, Jones headed up to see him for what would turn out to be the very last time:

> I went in there and when I started talking to him, of course, he got relaxed. He was laying in a hospital bed. . . . He didn't have a line in his face! He didn't have any wrinkles! He had white hair. I said, 'Richard, you look better without [the wig], to be honest with you. And you don't need make-up – your skin looks *fantastic*.'

The visit was the epilogue to a friendship cemented in 1969 when Richard appeared on the revue show *This Is Tom Jones*. With the Quasar draped in an orange smock, they tore through a rock'n'roll medley of tunes from his '50s pomp. The suits behind the scenes demurred at booking a musician they wrongly considered past his prime, but the Welsh don fought his hero's corner and was validated by a riotous performance. Richard changed the setlist seconds before plunging into the 1957 B-side 'Send Me Some Lovin'', leaving Jones's breathless band scrambling to keep up with the king of chaos.

Fifty years later, when Tom Jones visited Little Richard's hotel room, the medley had been uploaded to YouTube. At the time of writing, the clip has amassed more than four million views. 'I said, "People are still commenting on it!",' remembers Jones. 'And he said, "Oh, wonderful."'

Although Richard had insisted that no photos be taken that day, he ultimately posed for a quick phone snap with his pal, courtesy of Danny. He was often in pain towards the end of his life – from his ruined hip and, later, from the bone cancer that finally took him – yet, in that picture, he's looking up at Jones with unfettered warmth, care and love. He radiates positivity, appearing untouched by his troubles, which, in reality, deep down, cannot have been the case.

It's what he'd been doing since childhood: rising above the pain in his life to transmit a defiant kind of joy. He might have struggled to be Little Richard again after the era that produced his sensational debut album, but really he was someone even more interesting all along: Richard Penniman.

And after all these words about the King and Queen of Rock'n'roll, perhaps Dave Grohl puts it best when he says: 'He just had a fucking swing, man. And I just love that he was so larger-than-life. Visually, aesthetically. I just always considered him to be the baddest motherfucker in the world.'

Acknowledgements

Thank you to Rosie for her endless generosity, unshakable support and what seems to be limitless patience (though this is often put to the test!). And, of course, for the all-important 'Rosie Day edit'.

Enormous thanks to Leah-Babb Rosenfeld and Rachel Moore at Bloomsbury, and to boice-Terrel Allen for giving the book such a close and thoughtful edit. Thank you to Tom Smith for sending me the 33 1/3 open submission call in the first place, Alex Flood for his brilliant idea to mine the *NME* archive, John Robinson for cracking it open and Paul Ward for the use of its images.

I am also eternally grateful to the following legends for their help in arranging interviews and/or providing resources: Polly Birbeck, Aaron Feterl, Ben King, Sam Roberts, Cassandra Hightower, Katerina Marka, Chloe Munts, James Windle and John Wirt.

Once again, I raise the Devil's horns to the amazing contributors who made this book rock'n'roll.

And finally: thank you to Sidney Raven, the living embodiment of *a-wop-bop-aloo-bop-alop-bam-boom*.

Bibliography

Books

Ashby, LeRoy, *With Amusement for All: A History of American Popular Culture since 1830*. Lexington: The University Press of Kentucky, 2012.

Bennett, Stephanie, *Johnny B. Bad: Chuck Berry and the Making of Hail! Hail! Rock 'n' roll*. Los Angeles: Rare Bird Books, 2019.

Brown, Craig, *One Two Three Four: The Beatles in Time*. London: 4th Estate, 2020.

Chilton, John, *Let the Good Times Roll: The Story of Louis Jordan and His Music*. Ann Arbor: The University of Michigan Press, 1997.

Guralnick, Peter, *Last Train to Memphis: The Rise of Elvis Presley*. Boston, New York and London: Little, Brown and Company, 1994.

James, David E., *Rock 'n' Film: Cinema's Dance with Popular Music*. New York: Oxford University Press, 2016.

John, Elton, *Me: Elton John*. London: Pan Books, 2020.

Jordan, Martha with Coleman PhD, Edith A., *'The Debutante that Went Astray': An Autobiography of Martha Mrs. Louis Jordan*. Lee's Summit: E.L.M Institute Publishers, 2005.

Kirby, David, *Little Richard: The Birth of Rock 'n' roll*. New York: Continuum, 2011.

Koch, Stephen, *Louis Jordan: Son of Arkansas, Father of R&B*. Charleston: The History Press, 2014.

Lhamon, W. T., *Deliberate Speed: The Origins of a Cultural Style in the American 1950s*. Cambridge, MA and London: Harvard University Press, 1990.

Norman, Phillip, *John Lennon: The Life*. London: Harper, 2009.

Packard, Jerrold M., *American Nightmare: The History of Jim Crow*. New York: St. Martin's Press, 2002.

Ribowsky, Mark, *The Big Life of Little Richard*. The United States of America: Diversion Books, 2020.

Shaw, Arnold, *Honkers and Shouters: The Golden Years of Rhythm and Blues*. New York: Collier Books, 1978.

Tosche, Nick, *Unsung Heroes of Rock 'n' roll*. New York: De Capo Press, 1999.

Trynka, Paul, *Starman: David Bowie – The Definitive Biography*. London: Sphere, 2011.

Vera, Billy, *Rip It Up: The Specialty Records Story*. The United States of America: BMG Books, 2019.

White, Charles, *The Life and Times of Little Richard: The Authorized Biography*. London, New York, Paris, Sydney, Copenhagen, Berlin, Madrid and Tokyo: Omnibus Press, 2003.

Articles

'Art Rupe obituary', *The Times*, April 18, 2022.

Bassett, Jordan, 'The Story of Specialty Records, the Most Influential Label of all Time: "Songs Never Die"', *NME*, 3 August 2021, https://www.nme.com/features/music-features/rip-it-up-the-best-of-specialty-records-75th-anniversary-little-richard-3006616.

Brown, Tanya Bollard, 'The Origin (and Hot Stank) of the "Chitlin" Circuit', *NPR*, 16 February 2014, https://www.npr.org/sections

/codeswitch/2014/02/16/275313723/the-origin-and-hot-stank
   -of-the-chitlin-circuit.

Browne, David, 'Little Richard, Founding Father of Rock Who
   Broke Musical Barriers, Dead at 87', *Rolling Stone*, 9 May 2020,
   https://www.rollingstone.com/music/music-news/little-richard
   -dead-48505/.

Chalmers, Robert, 'Legend: Little Richard', *GQ*, 29 March 2012,
   https://www.gq-magazine.co.uk/article/gq-men-of-the-year
   -2010-little-richard-legend.

Dalton, David, 'Little Richard: Child of God', *Rolling Stone*, 28 May
   1970, https://www.rollingstone.com/music/music-features/little
   -richard-child-of-god-2-177027/.

'Drum Legend Charles Connor Keeps on Knockin'', *Goldmine*, 12
   November 2009, https://www.goldminemag.com/articles/drum
   -legend-charles-connor-keeps-on-knockin.

'Gene Vincent Introduces (and He Will in the Show) His Old Pal
   Little Richard', *The New Musical Express*, 5 October 1962.

Goodwin, Keith, 'He's Never Made a Record That Wasn't a Hit!'
   The New Musical Express, 20 September 1957.

Goodwin, Keith, 'Here's – Little Richard!' *The New Musical
   Express*, 29 March 1957.

Gray, Michael, 'Fats Domino Obituary: A Giant of American
   Music', *The Guardian*, 25 October 2017, https://www
   .theguardian.com/music/2017/oct/25/fats-domino-obituary.

Kriticos, Christian, 'Alis Lesley: "The Female Elvis" Who Takes
   Centre Stage on Bob Dylan's New Book Cover', *The Guardian*,
   21 October 2022, https://www.theguardian.com/music/2022/
   oct/21/alis-lesley-the-female-elvis-who-takes-centre-stage-on
   -bob-dylans-new-book-cover.

Lee, Christina, 'The Chitlin' Circuit Still Exists', *Red Bull Music
   Academy*, 30 January 2017, https://daily.redbullmusicacademy
   .com/2017/01/chitlin-circuit-feature.

'Little Richard Is Scent', *Melody Maker*, 6 July 1957.

'Little Richard with the Big Hair Hair-do', *The New Musical Express*, 9 November 1956.

Nyong'o, Tavia, 'Too Black, Too Queer, Too Holy: Why Little Richard Never Truly Got His Dues', *The Guardian*, 12 May 2020, https://www.theguardian.com/music/2020/may/12/too-black-queer-holy-why-little-richard-never-truly-got-his-dues-turbaned-drag-queen-sexual-underworld.

Mellon, Steve, 'Breaking records for the war effort', The Pittsburgh Post-Gazette, November 18, 2013. https://newsinteractive.post-gazette.com/thedigs/2013/11/18/breaking-records-for-the-war-effort/

O'Brien, Steve, 'A Shock to the System: How TV Tried to Tame Elvis', *Vintage Rock*, August/September 2021.

O'Brien, Steve, 'In Living Colour', *Vintage Rock Presents: The Rock 'n' roll Years Volume Two*, 2021.

O'Dell, Cary, '"Tutti Frutti" – Little Richard (1955)', *Library of Congress*, https://www.loc.gov/static/programs/national-recording-preservation-board/documents/TuttiFrutti.pdf.

Petridis, Alexis, 'Fats Domino: A Huge Talent Who Inspired the Beatles, Ska and Bling', *The Guardian*, 26 October 2017, https://www.theguardian.com/music/2017/oct/25/fats-domino-giant-talent-inspired-ska-beatles-bling-89-boogie-woogie.

Porterfield, Carlie, 'How Little Richard Was Exploited by a Bad Record Deal and Never Fully Cashed In', *Forbes*, 9 May 2020, https://www.forbes.com/sites/carlieporterfield/2020/05/09/how-little-richard-was-exploited-by-a-bad-record-deal-and-never-fully-cashed-in/?sh=7b77e8de4d96.

Roberts, Chris, 'Little Richard Ain't a Rocker Any More . . . God Put Out the Fire', *Melody Maker*, 13 October 1962.

Sacher, Andrew, 'David Bowie: "Without Little Richard, Myself and Half of My Contemporaries Wouldn't Be Playing Music"', *Brooklyn Vegan*, 9 May 2020, https://www.brooklynvegan.com

/david-bowie-without-little-richard-myself-and-half-of-my
-contemporaries-wouldnt-be-playing-music/.

Savage, Mark. 'Little Richard: What Did "A-wop-bop-a-loo-bop"
Actually Mean?', *BBC News*, 9 May 2020, https://www.bbc.co.uk
/news/entertainment-arts-52601898.

'Shock for Rock 'n' Roll World – Little Richard Packs It Up!' *The
New Musical Express*, 8 November 1957.

Scherman, Tony, 'Ding-Ding-Ding-Ding! That's the Way Rock
Began', The New York Times, April 25, 1999, https://www.
nytimes.com/1999/04/25/arts/music-ding-ding-ding-ding-
that-s-the-way-rock-began.html

Slim, Almost, 'Dorothy LaBostrie –The Woman Behind the Music',
Wavelength, November, 1984.

Watkins, Jack, 'Here's Little Richard', *Vintage Rock Presents: The
Rock 'n' roll Years Volume Two*, 2021.

Weiner, Tim, 'Little Richard, Flamboyant Wild Man of Rock
'n' Roll, Dies at 87', *New York Times*, May 2020, https://www
.nytimes.com/2020/05/09/arts/music/little-richard-dead.html.

West, David, 'Rocket Men', Vintage Rock, August/September 2021.

Williams, DeWitt S., 'Little Richard and His Time at Oakwood
College', *Spectrum Magazine*, 15 May 2020, https://
spectrummagazine.org/news/2020/little-richard-and-his-time
-oakwood-college.

Wirt, John, 'Little Richard: The Originator, the Emancipator, the
Architect of Rock 'n' roll', *The Advocate*, 16 January 1998.

Wirt, John, 'Little Richard Was Rocking Baton Rouge in the '50s',
The Advocate, 16 January 1998.

Other

50 Years of Little Richard. BBC Radio 4 broadcast, 11 November 2008.

Awards Show Network, 'American Bandstand 1964 – Interview Little Richard', YouTube Video, 3.23, 23 August 2017, https://www.youtube.com/watch?v=VjARpbNjFkw.

BBC Archive, '1972: LITTLE RICHARD Interview Is the GOAT | Late Night Line-Up | Classic BBC Music | BBC Archive', YouTube Video, 20 December 2021, https://www.youtube.com/watch?v=Btdzp52AmsE.

Coleman, Rick, 'Little Richard: The Specialty Sessions', Liner notes for *Little Richard: The Specialty Sessions*. ACE / Speciality Records/ ABOXLP1, 1989, LP.

Marcus Bona, 'Tom Jones and Little Richard - Rock 'n' Roll Medley - (1969) (Live)', YouTube Video, 5.54, 5 September 2016, https://www.youtube.com/watch?v=hiw9g3mG040.

'Rock and Roll; Renegades; Interview with Dorothy LaBostrie', GBH Archives, http://openvault.wgbh.org/catalog/V_CF6582A FE3E0492587D87B54983733F7, accessed 16 January 2022.

Specialty Records, 'Little Richard Is Tops', advertisement reproduced in *Billboard* article 'Here's Little Richard's Earliest Mentions in Billboard: "The Disk Is Going Like a Streak of Lightning"', 21 May 2020, https://www.billboard.com/music/music-news/little -richard-read-earliest-mentions-billboard-magazine-9387999/.

The Girl Can't Help It (1956), [Film] Dir. Frank Tashlin, USA, 20th Century Fox.

The Godmother of Rock 'n' Roll – Sister Rosetta Tharpe (2011), [Film] Dir. Mick Csaky, Antelope Films.

Warren, Sean, 'Little Richard – 1988 Grammy Awards Best New Artist–Jody Watley', YouTube Video, 16 October 2019, https://www.youtube.com/watch?v=wYvUDkfBAIQ.

Waters, John, 'John Waters on "The Girl Can't Help It"', 2004 DVD extra, *The Girl Can't Help It* (1956), [Film] Dir. Frank Tashlin, USA, 20th Century Fox.

Also available in the series

ALSO AVAILABLE IN THE SERIES

ALSO AVAILABLE IN THE SERIES